P9-CED-131

98.0974
S

J
700.9031
Hal

HALLIWELL, SARAH, editor

THE RENAISSANCE : ARTISTS AND
WRITERS

WHO AND WHEN?

The RENAISSANCE

Artists and Writers

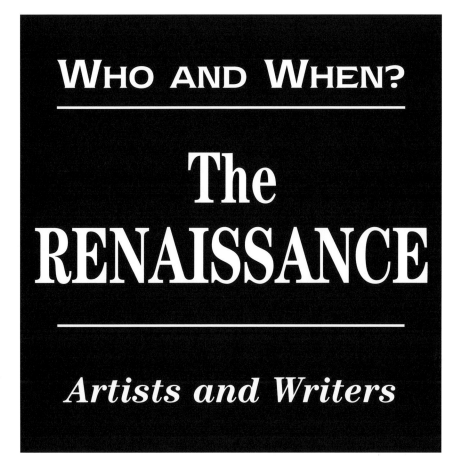

WHO AND WHEN?

The RENAISSANCE

Artists and Writers

Edited by Sarah Halliwell

RSVP
**RAINTREE
STECK-VAUGHN**
P U B L I S H E R S
The Steck-Vaughn Company

Austin, Texas

Steck-Vaughn Company

First published 1998 by Raintree Steck-Vaughn Publishers,
an imprint of Steck-Vaughn Company.
Copyright © 1998 Marshall Cavendish Limited.

Library of Congress Cataloging-in-Publication Data
The Renaissance: artists and writers/edited by Sarah Halliwell
p. cm. -- (Who and When: v. 1)
Includes bibliographical references and index.
Summary: Defines the main characteristics of early, high, and northern Renaissance art
and literature, focusing on thirteen artists, including Uccello, Michelangelo, and Brueghel,
and three authors: Dante, Chaucer, and Cervantes.
ISBN 0-8172-4725-4
1. Arts, Renaissance -- Juvenile literature. 2. Artists -- Biography -- Juvenile literature. [1. Arts,
Renaissance. 2. Artists. 3. Authors.] I. Halliwell, Sarah. II. Series.
NX450.5.R38 1998
700'.9'031--dc21   97-13925
                                                                                                              CIP
                                                                                                              AC

Printed and bound in Italy
1 2 3 4 5 6 7 8 9 0 LE 02 01 00 99 98 97

Marshall Cavendish Limited
Managing Editor: Ellen Dupont
Project Editor: Sarah Halliwell
Senior Editor: Andrew Brown
Senior Designer: Richard Newport
Designer: Richard Shiner
Picture administrator: Vimu Patel
Production: Craig Chubb
Index: Ella J. Skene

Raintree Steck-Vaughn
Publishing Director: Walter Kossmann
Project Manager: Joyce Spicer
Editor: Shirley Shalit

Consultants:
Anthea Peppin, National Gallery, London;
Dr. Andrew Hadfield, University of Wales;
Jonathan Kulp, University of Texas.

Contributors:
Ann Kay, Charles Phillips, Andrew Brown.

CONTENTS

INTRODUCTION

The term *Renaissance* comes from the French word meaning "rebirth." It refers to the flowering of the arts that began in Italy in the early 1300s and continued into the 16th century. The age had two main characteristics: the revival of an interest in the art and ideas of the ancient Greek and Roman worlds, and the growing respect for the individual. At the same time, attitudes toward religion were changing. Before, art had been a way of communicating religion to the people. But during the Renaissance, artists and writers became more aware of the world around them, and more interested in celebrating everyday human life.

Knowledge of the ancient world had not entirely disappeared. Several handwritten Greek and Roman manuscripts had survived into the 14th century. But most people could not read. The few who could were often churchmen, who did not want to promote the learning of pagan, or non-Christian, civilizations. The situation changed after the invention of printing in the 15th century, however. Now that books were quicker and cheaper to make, texts became more widely available, giving more people the opportunity to read.

The revival of early learning was particularly strong in Italy. This was partly because people could still see the ruined splendors of ancient Rome, and this reminded them of their capital city's former glory. The increased demand for art and literature was also a result of the political state of the country. Italy was not a unified nation, but a collection of small, fiercely competitive city-states, each ruled by a separate family. The rivalry of these families extended far beyond military matters. The leading Renaissance rulers—the Medicis, the Sforzas, the Estes—wanted to be known for their culture and learning, as much as for their strength. To show off their taste and wealth, they competed to employ the finest artists to decorate their extravagant palaces. These artists would often produce works taken from Greek and Roman myths and history to reflect their patrons' knowledge of the ancient world.

The increased demand for art signaled a shift in the social standing of artists. Until this time, people had considered artists as nothing more than humble craftsmen. No one knew their name, and people thought their work was no more valuable than that of a carpenter or a builder. But during the Renaissance, the idea of the creative genius was born, and a new admiration evolved for artists and writers.

People began to take notice of painters, who started to sign their pictures with pride. Michelangelo Buonarroti and Raphael (*see pages 56 and 62*) earned such fame and respect during their lifetimes that each became known as *il divino*— "the divine one." The 16th-century painter and writer, Giorgio Vasari, produced an account of the lives of the most famous artists, the first book of its kind.

Previously, the main role of art had been to illustrate Bible stories. Now, however, artists produced lifelike views of their own world. Painters used recent discoveries in anatomy and mathematics to help them portray the human figure more accurately. They also experimented with a new technique called "perspective" to represent depth and distance on a flat surface. This allowed them to create more realistic scenes.

These attempts to make art more closely related to the real world were echoed in the field of literature. Writers such as Geoffrey Chaucer and Miguel de Cervantes (*see pages 84 and 88*) presented a colorful and perceptive view of the societies in which they lived. Dante Alighieri (*see page 80*) was one of the first writers to work in the everyday language of the common man rather than in Latin, the language of scholars and the Church, which writers had normally used before.

The Renaissance is divided into several periods. "Early Renaissance" refers to the 14th and early 15th centuries, when artists such as Paolo Uccello and Masaccio (*see pages 18 and 24*) were developing new styles. "High Renaissance" describes the brief period from around 1500 to 1520, when the movement was at its peak. Leonardo da Vinci, Michelangelo, and Raphael (*see pages 46, 56, and 62*) were the stars of this high point. "Northern Renaissance" refers to the artistic developments made in northern Europe. Its leading figures—Hieronymus Bosch, Albrecht Dürer, and Pieter Brueghel (*see pages 40, 52, and 74*)—came from Germany and the Netherlands. The advances made in the north tended to follow those of Italy.

With such a variety of different times, places, and styles, it is impossible to give a single definition that covers all the diverse art and literature created during the Renaissance. But both the new awareness of the artist as an individual and the attempts to make art more realistic help explain why many historians see the Renaissance as the beginning of the modern age.

GIOTTO DI BONDONE

From humble beginnings, Giotto rose to become the leading painter of his day. His realistic and dramatic religious paintings set new standards in western art, and provided an inspiration for later artists.

Giotto di Bondone was the first painter to become a famous celebrity in his lifetime. Very little is known about his early life, however. Most information comes from the Renaissance poet, Dante Alighieri (*see page 80*), and the artist and writer, Giorgio Vasari, who wrote Giotto's biography two hundred years after the painter's death.

EARLY LIFE

It is thought that Giotto was born around 1267, in Colle di Vespignano, a village northeast of Florence, in central Italy. His father was a poor peasant farmer. As a boy, Giotto often looked after his father's sheep in the hills above his village. Legend has it that one day, while he was watching the flock, he amused himself by drawing a sheep on a piece of rock. As he was doing this, a painter called Cimabue passed by. He was amazed by Giotto's skill, and he at once took the boy on as his pupil.

Cimabue was the leading painter in Florence. He was moving away from the most common art of the time—flat-looking religious images—toward a style that made the people in his pictures seem more realistic.

Giotto's apprenticeship with Cimabue was short. Around 1280, his master went to the central Italian town of Assisi to work in the church of San Francesco, the burial place of St. Francis. Giotto probably stayed in Florence, visiting Rome a few years later to study the city's classical sculpture and early Christian wall paintings.

GROWING REPUTATION

By this time, Giotto had acquired a reputation of his own. Around 1287, when Cimabue returned to Florence, Giotto seems to have moved to Assisi to work in the San Francesco church. He was probably now an independent artist, perhaps with his own assistants.

Giotto di Bondone, by Paolo Uccello
The 15th-century artist, Uccello, painted this undated portrait as part of an panel entitled *The Founders of Florentine Art*.

Giotto probably spent the next 12 years painting the scenes from the life of St. Francis that decorate the walls of the upper church of San Francesco. Giotto's sensitive and expressive portrayal of St. Francis helped to shape the saint's image for hundreds of years.

In 1301, Giotto was back in Florence. Ten years earlier, he had married a Florentine woman, Ricevuta di Lapo del Pela, known as Ciuta. The couple would have eight children. Giotto bought a house for his family in

> "It was Giotto alone who, by God's favor, rescued and restored the art of painting ...."
> (Giorgio Vasari)

Florence, and now settled down to a life of domestic bliss. Before long, however, he was summoned north to Padua, where he received an important commission from Enrico Scrovegni, one of the town's wealthiest citizens.

CHAPEL MASTERPIECE

Scrovegni's father had become rich by lending money at a very high rate of interest. This practice—known as "usury"—was regarded as sinful at the time. To pay for his father's sins and to restore the family's good name, Enrico built a small chapel next to the family

SAINT FRANCIS

Giotto took as his subject the life of Francis of Assisi, perhaps one of the best-loved of saints.

Francis was born in 1181 or 1182 in Assisi, central Italy, where his father was a wealthy cloth merchant. As a rich young man, Francis liked to have lots of fun. But in 1204, after a severe illness, he became very religious. He gave away everything he owned, including all his clothes and money. He then began to live an extremely simple life, owning nothing but an old tunic.

Francis dedicated his life to copying Christ in all things. He helped the poor and sick, and spread the word of God all around. He loved all God's creatures, especially animals. In Giotto's San Francesco frescoes

palace. The Arena Chapel, named for the Roman amphitheater on whose site it stood, was consecrated in 1305. Shortly after, Scrovegni gave Giotto the job of decorating the chapel walls.

Appropriately, the theme of Giotto's wall paintings was the salvation of humankind from sin. The main scenes represented episodes from the life of Joachim and Anna—the parents of the

(*above*), the artist showed the gentle Saint Francis preaching to the birds.

Francis attracted many loyal followers, and in 1209, he established an order of friars, the Franciscans, which still exists today. Francis died in 1226, and two years later, Pope Gregory IX declared him a saint.

Virgin Mary—the life of Mary herself, and the life of Jesus.

Beneath these, Giotto painted the Vices and Virtues, or representations of bad and good behavior. He painted these in gray so they looked like stone carvings. Over the chapel entrance, he illustrated *The Last Judgment*—a story in the Bible in which God separates the good people from the bad.

Giotto's Arena Chapel pictures marked a departure from anything that had gone before. No previous artist had made the figures in his paintings look so three-dimensional and solid, or portrayed human emotions so vividly and convincingly.

Rather than following the ideas of earlier artists, Giotto developed a completely new way of painting his biblical scenes. He tried to visualize what the events must have really looked like as they happened. He tried to show how the characters would have reacted to the dramatic situations: how they would have stood, acted, and moved. Unlike earlier artists, who painted flat, unrealistic figures on gold backgrounds, Giotto set his dramas in natural landscapes, and used light and shade to make his figures seem more solid and real. He carefully modeled faces and painted clothes full of deep folds.

A SIMPLE VISION

Giotto went straight to the heart of the story and illustrated it with just a few elements. He expressed emotions not through violent movements, but through simple gestures. He placed the main figures at the front of his pictures. This not only brought them closer to the viewer but also allowed Giotto to tell the story more clearly.

Giotto realized that the eyes and mouth are the most expressive parts of the human face. By emphasizing these features, he was able to represent powerful and intense emotion. In *The Lamentation of Christ*, for example, the Virgin's face is contorted with pain

The Lamentation of Christ, c.1303-05, by Giotto di Bondone
This is one of Giotto's most famous frescoes. He expresses with shocking realism the overwhelming despair of the Virgin Mary as she cradles her lifeless son in her arms.

after the death of her son, while, above, angels fill the sky with their wails of grief.

FRESCO PAINTING

The Arena Chapel wall paintings were done in a technique called *fresco*, in which the paint was applied to fresh wet plaster: The word fresco is Italian for "fresh." The plaster dried in a few hours, and the paint became a part of the wall rather than merely being on its surface. This meant that the picture would not flake off.

But the technique also made it hard for the artist to make changes. Once the plaster had dried, errors could be corrected only by chipping away plaster and starting again, or by repainting on patches of dry plaster, which produced less permanent results. Fresco painting therefore demanded a bold and confident approach from the artist. He had to have a clear vision of the forms he wanted and a sure hand to be able to express them swiftly and accurately. Although close examination of the Arena Chapel shows several small alterations, Giotto painted most of his forms quickly, easily, and precisely.

RICH AND FAMOUS

Word of Giotto's achievement quickly spread throughout Italy. He returned to Florence to find himself famous. In his *Divine Comedy*, Dante hailed Giotto as the greatest living artist. For the next 20 years, Giotto worked mainly in the city of Florence.

Around the 1320s, Giotto probably painted frescoes in four chapels in the Florentine church of Santa Croce. Those in the Bardi Chapel on the life of St. Francis are among his most expressive and influential works.

Giotto was now a wealthy man. He lent money, and bought and sold land. He was a kind and witty person and also very confident of his own abilities. According to one story, Pope Benedict XI wanted to commission frescoes for the great Church of St. Peter in Rome and he sent a messenger to Giotto to find out what his work was like. Giotto drew a single circle on a sheet of paper and sent the man back with it. The circle was so perfect that Giotto's great skill was obvious to the pope at once.

Other powerful patrons were also aware of his talents. In 1328, the king of Naples summoned Giotto to work in his palace. Giotto adapted easily to the court, and was on familiar terms with the king. When the king announced that he wanted to make Giotto the "first man" in Naples, the artist replied that, as he lived right at the city gate, he was already the first man.

By 1334, however, Giotto was back in Florence, where his career took an unexpected turn. He was appointed architect of Florence Cathedral. He was also given responsibility for building the city walls. It was a surprising appointment. It is unlikely that Giotto had any architectural experience. During the Renaissance, however, patrons often expected artists to turn their hand to anything connected with design.

A LASTING REPUTATION

The cathedral was already under construction, and Giotto supervised the raising of the magnificent campanile, or bell tower. This is Giotto's last known work. He died on January 8, 1337. He was buried in Florence Cathedral, an unprecedented honor for a painter. His reputation lived on. Over a century later, a tomb was erected in his memory. Its epitaph proclaimed, "I am the man who raised painting from the dead."

MAJOR WORKS

c.1290-96	LIFE OF ST. FRANCIS FRESCO CYCLE, ASSISI
c.1305-06	ARENA CHAPEL FRESCO CYCLE, PADUA
c.1305-10	OGNISSANTI MADONNA
c. 1325	LIFE OF ST. FRANCIS FRESCOES, SANTA CROCE
c.1334	FLORENCE CAMPANILE (BELL TOWER)

JAN VAN EYCK

One of the most famous artists in the history of the Netherlands, van Eyck improved the technique of oil painting. His mastery of the medium led later writers to describe him as "the king of painters."

In spite of his fame, very little is known about Jan van Eyck's life. He was probably born around 1390, in Maaseyck, a small town near Maastricht, in the southern Netherlands.

DIPLOMAT AND COURTIER

The first certain record of the artist dates from 1422. In that year, he was in The Hague, a major city in the Netherlands, working as painter and personal servant to the Count of Holland, John of Bavaria. John died in 1425, but van Eyck found new employment with Philip the Good, the duke of Burgundy. He traveled to Philip's court in Lille—now in northern France—to take up his position. As the court artist, van Eyck's work ranged from painting portraits to designing costumes and ornaments for festivities. He had to paint shields and banners, color statues, and even create elaborate dishes for court banquets.

Van Eyck also went on a number of important diplomatic missions for Philip. In 1426, he took part in a pilgrimage in his employer's place, and also went on "a secret mission" for the duke. Over the next ten years, he undertook several similar tasks.

In 1433, around a year after buying a house in Bruges, a town on the coast of modern Belgium, van Eyck got married. His wife was called Margaret, but we know little else about her. The couple had at least two children.

THE GHENT ALTARPIECE

Van Eyck's earliest known picture, the *Ghent Altarpiece*, dates from 1432. His brother, Hubert, who was also a painter, had begun this huge work for the cathedral in Ghent, a town near Bruges, but had left it unfinished when he died in around 1426. Jan probably started work on completing the picture sometime in the late 1420s.

Jan van Eyck, by Joachim von Sandrart **This 17th-century copper engraving is undated. It is thought to be a copy of a contemporary likeness of the artist.**

The Madonna and Child with Chancellor Rolin, c.1435, by Jan van Eyck
Van Eyck shows Chancellor Nicolas Rolin, one of the most important of Philip the Good's officials, devotedly praying before the Virgin and Child.

The painting's theme was Jesus' sacrifice. In one panel, worshippers kneel before a lamb, a traditional symbol for Jesus. The work was greatly admired by van Eyck's contemporaries, and has continued to impress artists and critics through the centuries. The German artist, Albrecht Dürer (*see page 52*), called it a "stupendous painting."

Van Eyck also had a major impact on the development of the portrait. Before him, many artists exaggerated their models' features. He, however, used a more naturalistic style—in which people and objects appeared more as they would in the real world. He had a keen eye for everyday detail and had a gift for reproducing the appearance of wrinkled skin, fur, or shining metal. He reproduced the features of one sitter so precisely that modern doctors can tell which disease he was suffering from.

Sometimes, van Eyck combined several types of picture in one work. In around 1435, for example, he painted a portrait of Chancellor Rolin of Burgundy. To underline the chancellor's religious faith, van Eyck shows him kneeling before the Virgin Mary, who has the child Jesus on her lap. Beyond the figures are three ornate arches, through which appears a highly detailed landscape showing a river and a city. From this landscape, it seems the artist had a basic knowledge of perspective, a new technique developed in Italy for representing depth and distance in a painting. At the time, perspective was not widely known in northern Europe.

COLORS IN OIL

For many years, people thought van Eyck had invented oil painting. But artists had in fact used oil paints in a limited way for some time. He was, however, the first to show their true potential. Oil paints are those in which the colors, or pigments, are mixed with oil. In van Eyck's day, most artists used tempera, a mixture of pigment, egg, and water, which dried quickly and was difficult to use. Van Eyck also used tempera, but on top of this he applied layers of oil paint. The oil in the mixture reflected light, giving his colors a rich, intense glow.

PERSONAL MARKS

In many works, van Eyck included inscriptions, either on the frame or in the painting. He used the phrase "As best I can" on several occasions. In his most famous work, *The Arnolfini Marriage*," he left his mark by writing in Latin "Jan van Eyck was here, 1434." The picture—a portrait of a couple standing in a bedchamber—was probably painted to record the marriage of an Italian merchant, Giovanni Arnolfini. It contained many objects that refer to their married state, such as a small dog, which symbolizes fidelity.

In the 1430s, van Eyck continued to work as a diplomat for Philip the Good. The duke still valued his art very highly, however. In 1435, he intervened when Jan's pension was not paid. He said that he did not want to lose the painter, as "we could find no other artist to our liking who is so accomplished."

Van Eyck died in Bruges, in 1441. He was around 50. In recognition of the artist's genius, Philip allowed him to be buried in the church of St. Donat, a traditional burial place for the nobility. The duke also granted van Eyck's widow an allowance "in consideration of her husband's services."

MAJOR WORKS

c.1425-32	THE GHENT ALTARPIECE
1433	PORTRAIT OF A MAN IN A RED TURBAN
1434	"THE ARNOLFINI MARRIAGE"
c.1435	THE MADONNA AND CHILD WITH CHANCELLOR ROLIN
c.1434-36	THE MADONNA WITH CANON VAN DER PAELE

PAOLO UCCELLO

One of the most inventive artists of the early Renaissance, Uccello dedicated his life to art. Neglecting his family and friends, he worked obsessively to represent depth, distance, and three dimensions on a flat picture surface.

Paolo Uccello was born in Florence, probably in 1397, although the exact date is uncertain. Paolo's original name was Paolo di Dono, but he became known as Uccello—the Italian word for "bird"—because he was very fond of birds. His father, Dono di Paolo, was a barber and a surgeon—during the Renaissance it was common for the same person to have both jobs.

A FAMOUS TEACHER

In 1407, Uccello joined the workshop of Lorenzo Ghiberti, then the most famous sculptor in Florence. It was an exciting time to work with Ghiberti. He was working on an important commission to make a pair of bronze doors for the city's baptistery, a task that took him more than 20 years to complete.

At first, Uccello's duties in the workshop would have been simple ones, such as sweeping the floor. But by the time he left in 1415, he had advanced so much that he was able to set up as an independent artist in his own right. He abandoned sculpture and switched to painting instead. It was not unusual at this time for artists to move between different branches of their trade, thus learning and practicing a wide range of skills. In the same year, Uccello joined a trade guild, or association. Membership of the guild gave him the right to open his own workshop and employ assistants. But he was a solitary man, and from this point he seems to have worked alone.

MASTERFUL MOSAICS

For the next ten years, Uccello worked as a painter in Florence. He may also have gained some experience of mosaics—pictures made from fragments of colored glass and marble. In 1425, the government of Venice, northeast Italy, summoned him to work on the mosaics in San Marco, the city's most important

Self-portrait, by Paolo Uccello
This undated picture was part of Uccello's panel *The Founders of Florentine Art*, which also showed the artist Giotto.

church. Documents from the project describe him as a "master mosaicist."

By 1431, Uccello was back in Florence. It was a time of great artistic activity in the city, and Uccello must have been anxious to find work. He did not have to wait for long. Soon, he began to produce some frescoes for Santa Maria Novella, a large church in Florence. These showed biblical scenes, such as *The Creation of Adam.*

These frescoes made Uccello's name. In 1436, he received a major commission from Florence Cathedral—to produce a portrait of the English *condottiere*, or mercenary commander, Sir John Hawkwood. At this time, Italy was made up of several rival city-states. Each city paid money to experienced soldiers to fight on its behalf against other cities. Hawkwood was one of the most famous to fight for Florence.

A LOVE OF PERSPECTIVE

In his portrait of Hawkwood, Uccello began to explore perspective. This technique, which the architect Filippo Brunelleschi had recently worked out, had revolutionized art. It made possible the representation on a flat surface of depth, distance, and three dimensions, by showing how objects become smaller as they get farther away.

When working on a picture, the artist imagined a number of diagonal lines, or orthogonals, which meet at a single "vanishing point." Wherever the artist placed an object along an orthogonal determined how big that object should be. For the first time, painters could show a scene as it really looked.

MEDICI PATRONAGE

One Florentine merchant family, the Medici, paid for some of the finest artworks of the Italian Renaissance.

For most of the period from the early 1400s to the mid-18th century, the Medici family dominated the political life of Florence and the surrounding area, Tuscany. The family originally arrived in Florence as immigrants in the 13th century, and made their fortune in banking and trade.

In 1434, Cosimo de' Medici (*above right*) became the virtual ruler of the city. Ten years later, he began construction of a large family palace. Cosimo's son, Piero de' Medici, commissioned Uccello to paint his celebrated series *The Battle of San Romano* to decorate the palace.

The great Renaissance sculptor Donatello was the first to use perspective successfully, and his pioneering work impressed his friend, Uccello. In fact, Uccello became obsessed with the technique. He was so dedicated that he would sit up all night working on drawings. When his wife, Tommasa, called him to bed, he would reply "Oh, what a wonderful thing is perspective!"

Uccello was not the only artist of the time to benefit from the patronage of the Medici. They were cultured individuals of great taste and encouraged excellence in all artistic and intellectual activities. They employed some of the most illustrious figures in the history of Italian art, including Donatello, Botticelli, and Michelangelo (see pages 34 and 56).

No one knows when Uccello married, but it is known that his wife gave birth to a boy in 1453. Uccello was in his mid-50s by this time, so his wife must have been much younger than her husband to bear a child. Three years later, the couple had a daughter, Antonia. She followed her father and worked as a painter. She was one of the few women artists of the Renaissance.

Uccello was a likable, but rather odd, character. In the late 1440s, he worked at the church of San Miniato al Monte in Florence, painting frescoes that showed what life in a monastery was like. According to Giorgio Vasari, who wrote the lives of many Renaissance artists, Uccello fled the job because the abbot only gave him cheese to eat. The artist said: "Your dim-witted abbot has filled me so full of cheese that I'm frightened he'll use me to make glue. If he carries on like this, I won't be Paolo Uccello any more, I'll be pure cheese!"

In 1445, Donatello asked Uccello to come to Padua, in northern Italy. Donatello was working there on a set of bronze carvings for the church of Sant' Antonio. Despite Uccello's training as a sculptor, he did not help on the project, but instead produced paintings for Padua's wealthy citizens.

Uccello returned to Florence around 1447, and began work on some more biblical frescoes for Santa Maria Novella. One of these, *The Flood*, illustrated the story of Noah, who built a large ship, or ark, to save his family and a collection of animals from a huge flood sent by God to punish sinners.

FAMOUS BATTLE SCENES

During the 1450s, Uccello worked on a commission to decorate the new palace of a powerful Florentine merchant family, the Medici. He produced a series of three large paintings commemorating the Battle of San Romano. This was a battle in 1432, at which Florence had conquered the nearby city of Siena.

St. George and the Dragon, c.1455-60, by Paolo Uccello
In this picture of St. George saving an elegant princess from a dragon, Uccello creates
the illusion of depth and distance by placing the edges of patches of grass along the lines
that lead to the vanishing point in the center of the picture.

In his *San Romano* pictures, Uccello showed his interest in perspective. Broken lances, scattered pieces of armor, and a dead soldier all pointed along the orthogonals, suggesting depth and distance. Uccello also made the soldiers and the horses look as if they really stand out in space and jump out of the picture. They seem to be carved from wood rather than painted in oils. He achieved similar effects in his *St. George and the Dragon*, which he painted around the same time.

FINAL DAYS

By the 1460s, Uccello's creativity was drying up. In 1465, he went to Urbino, in central Italy, to paint an altarpiece. But he returned to Florence three years later, leaving the work unfinished. He was now in his 70s, and in his tax return of August 1469 he grumbled: "I am old and without means of livelihood, my wife is ill, and I can no longer work."

Uccello lived for another six years. On December 10, 1475, he died, at the age of about 78. He was buried in the church of Santo Spirito in Florence.

MAJOR WORKS

c.1432	THE CREATION OF ADAM
1436	SIR JOHN HAWKWOOD
c.1447-50	THE FLOOD
c.1455-60	THE BATTLE OF SAN ROMANO; ST. GEORGE AND THE DRAGON
c.1460-65	THE HUNT AT NIGHT

MASACCIO

In his short life, Masaccio made several important innovations in the art of painting. His treatment of space and light influenced generations of Italian artists, earning him the title "Founder of the Renaissance."

Masaccio was born on the feast day of Saint Thomas, December 21, 1401. He was given the saint's name, Tommaso, but was later nicknamed Masaccio, or "clumsy Tom," because of his careless nature. Masaccio grew up in San Giovanni da Valdarno, a town in central Italy, but in around 1417, he moved with his family to Florence. The artistic city provided a stimulating environment for the young man. By the age of 20, he was an established independent painter.

EARLY INFLUENCES

Little is known of Masaccio's early training. He may have learned his skills from Masolino da Panicale, an artist from his own region, who would be his lifelong friend. One thing is clear, though: Masaccio was greatly influenced by the sculpture of ancient Greece and Rome. He also studied the paintings of Giotto (*see page 8*), which he admired for their uncluttered, solid simplicity and emotional power.

Masaccio's most important contacts in Florence were the architect Filippo Brunelleschi and the sculptor Donatello. Brunelleschi was at that time developing linear perspective, a system of showing depth on a flat surface. Donatello was trying to create the appearance of space in his sculptures.

Masaccio absorbed the lessons of Brunelleschi and Donatello. Even in his earliest works, he tackled the problem that was to dominate his short career: how to make his figures look natural, and the space around them seem real. In his first work, for example, an altarpiece for the church of San Giovenale in Florence dating from 1422, Masaccio painted the Madonna with a group of saints. Rather than floating on a flat gold background, as they tend to in paintings by earlier artists, these figures are solid, and fill a realistic space.

The Raising of the Son of Theophilus (detail), 1425-28, by Masaccio
This detail from one of the Brancacci frescoes is believed to be a self-portrait.

The Holy Trinity, 1427, by Masaccio
This masterpiece stunned people with its astonishing perspective.
As well as the trinity, it shows the Virgin and St. John standing
beneath Christ. The kneeling figures may have paid for the work.

In 1425, Antonio Brancacci, a very wealthy Florentine merchant, commissioned Masaccio and his friend Masolino to decorate his family's chapel with scenes from the life of St. Peter. Masaccio also painted an additional scene from the story of Adam and Eve, *The Expulsion from Paradise*. The wall decorations were painted in the technique known as fresco.

STUNNING INNOVATIONS

Masaccio's frescoes astonished people with their remarkable treatment of light and space. His figures appeared to stand out from the flat picture surface, an effect called foreshortening. His use of light effects gave the impression that light was shining on the picture from just one point. This caused the objects in the paintings to cast deep shadows, making them seem more weighty and three-dimensional. These innovations were greatly admired, and generations of Italian painters including Botticelli, Leonardo, Raphael, and, in particular, Michelangelo, would study them (*see pages 34, 46, 62, and 56*).

Word of Masaccio's work quickly spread, and he was soon receiving commissions from all over central Italy. He was so busy that he had no time for life outside work; he never married.

In 1427, he started work on *The Holy Trinity*, a fresco for the church of Santa Maria Novella in Florence. It showed God, Christ on the cross, and the Holy Spirit, represented by a white dove. For the work, Masaccio used Brunelleschi's system of perspective for the first time—in a striking way. He made the flat wall look like a hole opening into a long chapel.

In preparing the fresco, Masaccio used a cartoon, or a large drawing, fastened to the wall. The outline of the drawing was transferred to the plaster by puncturing it with pinpricks, or by rubbing charcoal into the holes, so a trace was left behind. This method later became very common, but Masaccio was probably the first to use it.

AN EARLY DEATH

In the summer of 1428, Masaccio was called to Rome, where he probably helped Masolino with frescoes for the church of San Clemente. But not long after his arrival, Masaccio died, ending his brilliant career at the age of just 26. His death was so sudden that there were rumors he had been poisoned. When the news reached Florence, Brunelleschi, shocked and grief-stricken, said that Masaccio's death was a great loss.

MAJOR WORKS

1422	SAN GIOVENALE TRIPTYCH
1424-25	MADONNA AND CHILD WITH ST. ANNE
1425-28	EXPULSION FROM PARADISE; THE TRIBUTE MONEY; DISTRIBUTION OF ALMS; ST. PETER HEALING THE SICK
1426	THE VIRGIN AND CHILD
1427	THE HOLY TRINITY

PIERO DELLA FRANCESCA

In his lifetime, Piero was respected as a mathematician and theorist as well as a painter. From the 17th century through the late 19th century, however, his calm, delicately colored paintings were largely neglected.

Piero was born in the small town of Borgo San Sepolcro—now known as Sansepolcro—about 40 miles southeast of Florence, Italy. There is no record of the exact date of his birth, but it was probably about 1415. His father, Benedetto, was a bootmaker and tanner—someone who turns animal skins into leather.

HUMBLE BEGINNINGS

Little is known about Piero's upbringing, but he clearly loved his birthplace, for although his career took him to several major art centers, he always returned to Sansepolcro. The town and the surrounding countryside appear in a number of his paintings.

Some sources mention Piero in connection with minor artistic jobs—such as painting candle poles used in church processions—from 1431 onward. Some of these documents state that payment was made through Piero's father, showing that Piero was still young at the time.

By 1439, Piero had moved on to more serious artistic work. In that year, he helped Domenico Veneziano, a highly regarded painter of the time, with frescoes in the church of San' Egidio in Florence. The city must have been an exciting place for the young artist, who would have found plenty of inspiration there, including the frescoes of Masaccio (*see page 24*).

FIRST MAJOR WORK

From Florence, Piero returned to his native Sansepolcro, where, in 1445, he received his first recorded independent commission for a major work. This was an altarpiece for the Compagnia della Misericordia—Brotherhood of Mercy, an organization dedicated to helping people, particularly the sick.

The central panel of this work shows a monumental Virgin holding her deep,

The Resurrection (detail), c.1460-65,
by Piero della Francesca
The writer Giorgio Vasari described this detail of a soldier as Piero's self-portrait.

blue cloak around several kneeling figures in a gesture of protection. Piero gives this traditional image a new clarity and boldness. He includes only the most vital information, and uses a limited number of colors.

A METHODICAL WORKER

Piero seems to have taken a very long time—17 years—to finish the Misericordia altarpiece. He was always a slow and deliberate worker. Piero carefully planned and constructed all his paintings down to the smallest detail; there is nothing casual or hurried about his art. With his subtle color harmonies and balanced compositions, he creates a sense of quiet, stillness, and calm. His figures, with their steady gazes, have all the monumental presence of ancient Greek and Egyptian statues.

THE AREZZO FRESCOES

Another reason why Piero took so long to complete his Misericordia altarpiece is that he was frequently called away to work in other places. The most important of his commissions was for a series of frescoes in the church of San Francesco, in Arezzo, where he worked during the 1450s.

The Legend of the True Cross series was commissioned by the Bacci family, who were merchants from Arezzo. An old-fashioned Florentine painter called Bicci di Lorenzo began the decoration of the Bacci family chapel in 1445, but died in 1452, before he had begun work on the walls. Piero took over and, with his assistants, spent most of the next 12 years on the task. The artist completed

PIERO AND PERSPECTIVE

Piero was a highly intelligent artist who exercised his inquisitive mind by writing on art and mathematics.

Piero was fascinated by perspective, which artists used to create the illusion of distance and depth in a painting. In earlier times, paintings looked very flat and artists struggled to create a space that looked realistic.

Perspective opened up an exciting new set of possibilities for artists. Painters such as Masaccio—one of the earliest to use the system—could make their figures inhabit a real space, and lead the viewer's eye back into the distance.

Piero understood and applied perspective techniques superbly, because he was a brilliant mathematician and took a keen

the work certainly by 1465, and probably by 1460.

The series is based on a set of medieval legends about the cross on which Jesus was crucified. The cross is supposed to have been made of wood that came from the Garden of Eden. According to the legend, the cross was rediscovered in the 4th century by St. Helena, and then figured in various

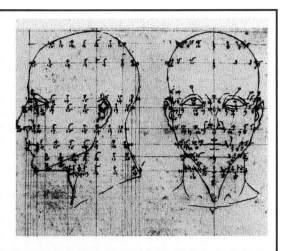

interest in the theory. During the last 20 years of his life, he wrote many treatises, the most famous of which was *De prospectiva pingendi*—On Perspective in Painting. In this work, Piero provided detailed diagrams to show how artists should represent objects and people on a flat surface (*above*).

Piero's written works were not fully published until the 20th century, but the number of manuscript copies of them shows that many people were familiar with his theory during the 16th century.

miracles. Piero's genius transformed this fanciful tale into some of the most solemn and serene images in the history of Christian art.

One of Piero's strengths was making the spiritual world accessible to his audience. Probably toward the end of his work at Arezzo, Piero painted the *Resurrection*. In this work, Piero used a stone parapet to separate the spiritual

world of Christ from the human soldiers. Yet he depicted Christ as a solid, heavy, muscular figure, rather than a remote, otherworldly image.

ADJUSTING TO FRESCO

The technique of fresco is one that was not naturally suited to such a slow worker as Piero. Since it is exceptionally durable, mistakes are difficult to correct, and so the artist has to get things right the first time. Piero ingeniously overcame this problem by applying wet cloths to the plaster at night, so he could continue working on the same section of wall for days, rather than the few hours it normally took the

> "Piero was ... fond of making clay models, which he would drape with wet cloths arranged in ... folds, and then use for drawing...."
> (Giorgio Vasari)

plaster to dry. The marks of the cloth can still be seen in places when the paintings are examined closely.

AT THE COURT OF URBINO

Piero worked at Ferrara, in northern Italy, and Rome. His paintings no longer survive in either place, however. He also

The Resurrection, c.1460-65, by Piero della Francesca
This fresco shows Christ risen from the dead standing over sleeping soldiers. According to Giorgio Vasari, this painting was considered Piero's finest.

worked in Urbino, which was ruled by Duke Federigo da Montefeltro, one of the most cultured art patrons of the Renaissance. The duke attracted many famous artists to work at his court, which was a famous center of learning and the arts.

There is only one known document referring to Piero's presence in Urbino, but he spent a good deal of time in the city, traveling there many times between 1450 and 1480. His Urbino pictures include one of his best-known works, *The Flagellation of Christ*.

This strange work reveals Piero's mastery of perspective—the scientific system used to create a sense of space and depth. The effect is heightened by Piero's careful attention to showing how light and shadows fall. We know from Piero's own writings that he achieved this accuracy though intense mathematical research. Even though no one knows for sure what this mysterious picture is about, its fine detail and overall harmony are greatly admired.

STRIKING PORTRAITS
Piero also produced a pair of portraits showing the Duke Federigo and his wife, Battista Sforza. In these works, which are among the most distinctive portraits of the Renaissance, Piero showed that he could capture the unique character of his sitter. Both the duke and his wife appear in profile against a landscape of wooded hills.

It was common in Italy at this time to portray sitters in profile. And Piero had a reason to adopt this format— Federigo had lost his right eye in a jousting tournament. Yet it was unusual to pay so much attention to the landscape in the background. Piero painted this with great sensitivity: The land is bathed in pale light.

SERENE FIGURES
The faces of Piero's characters are stylized, with a rounded, smoothed look. Although his men and women may look inexpressive at first, and nearly always seem to be thoughtful rather than active, they are serene and full of grace. Emotion and expression is simply hinted at, rather than portrayed openly. This helps to create the sense of stillness and purity in his art.

LOSING HIS SIGHT
Piero's eyesight evidently got worse in his old age. When he made his will in 1487, he declared himself "sound in mind, in intellect, and in body," but there is no record of him painting for about a decade before this. Perhaps his sight was good enough for reading and writing, but not for painting.

Instead of art, Piero seems to have devoted his later years to studying mathematics and perspective. He wrote pamphlets about these subjects. Piero's love of mathematical logic, order, and clarity shows in the graceful way in which he composed his paintings.

Piero died in Sansepolcro in 1492, probably in his late 70s. He was unmarried and had no children. He left his property to his brothers.

MAJOR WORKS

c.1445	MADONNA OF THE MISERICORDIA
1450s	THE BAPTISM OF CHRIST
c.1450-60	THE FLAGELLATION OF CHRIST
1452-60	THE LEGEND OF THE TRUE CROSS
c.1460-65	THE RESURRECTION
c.1465	PORTRAIT OF FEDERIGO DA MONTEFELTRO
c.1470-75	THE NATIVITY

SANDRO BOTTICELLI

Forgotten for hundreds of years, Botticelli's genius was rediscovered in the mid-19th century. During his own lifetime, Botticelli's beautiful and distinctive style brought him fame throughout Italy.

Sandro Botticelli was born Alessandro di Mariano Filipepi in around 1445. His plump elder brother had the nickname "*il Botticello,*" which means "little barrel." The rest of the Filipepi family, including the artist, later adopted this as their surname.

RENAISSANCE FLORENCE

Alessandro was born in the most exciting city of the Renaissance—Florence. His father was a tanner. He grew up in the bustle of Florence's Ognissanti, or All Saints, district, which was full of tanners and weavers. Botticelli would stay in this relatively poor area all his life.

Little is known about the artist's early years. What is certain is that he wanted to be a painter from an early age. By 1462, he was working in the workshop of the famous artist Fra Filippo Lippi, who specialized in religious paintings and gentle Madonnas. When the master died, in 1469, his son Filippino became Botticelli's pupil.

Botticelli quickly established himself as a promising young artist, working from his studio in the family home. Prestigious commissions were soon flooding in. In 1470, he received his first known commission: to paint one of the seven virtues—Fortitude—to adorn the walls of the Merchant's Guild, a Renaissance trade association.

By the time Botticelli was 30, he had produced paintings such as *The Adoration of the Magi*, commissioned to hang in the Florentine church of Santa Maria Novella. Such works came to the attention of the Medici family.

The wealthy and powerful Medicis ruled the thriving city of Florence at this time. They were great art lovers and their favor could make—or break—an artist's reputation. Botticelli may have painted his famous *Primavera*—Spring—for the Medicis, in about 1478.

The Adoration of the Magi (detail), c.1475, by Sandro Botticelli
Botticelli depicted himself behind the three kings visiting the newborn Christ.

While Botticelli prospered under the Medici's favor, other people in the city were unhappy with Medici rule. In the late 1470s, there was an assassination attempt on the ruler himself, Lorenzo de' Medici, known as "the Magnificent." But he escaped, and those who had been plotting against the Medicis were hunted down and hanged. Botticelli was asked to paint the dead men's pictures.

SUCCESS IN FLORENCE

By the early 1480s, Botticelli had become the star of Florence, sought out by all the grandest families in this glittering Renaissance city. The city government and Florentine churches also commissioned him, and so he produced an endless stream of paintings, religious and secular—worldly—on a wide variety of different subjects.

His paintings of the Madonna and Child were especially popular. People may even have bought them directly from the artist's workshop. Botticelli's reputation was helped by the fact that the city's greatest painter, Leonardo da Vinci (*see page 46*), had moved away to Milan. His fame had spread elsewhere in Italy, too. In 1481, Pope Sixtus IV commissioned him to decorate his new chapel in the Vatican Palace.

A LIVELY WORKSHOP

Botticelli's workshop became a thriving, highly productive place, where assistants made their own versions of Botticelli's work—a standard practice in Renaissance times. Since the artist himself only signed one of his paintings—*The Mystic Nativity*—this makes

THE SISTINE CHAPEL

Rome's famous chapel was decorated by some of the greatest Renaissance artists—including Botticelli.

The dynamic Sixtus IV, pope between 1471 and 1484, was responsible for many of Rome's finest buildings, which would never have been built without his love of art. He also had countless churches in the city repaired during his rule. Perhaps his greatest triumph of all was the construction of a chapel in the papal Vatican Palace—the Sistine Chapel (*right*).

The building of the Sistine Chapel was completed in 1481, when Botticelli was approaching the peak of his fame. Pope Sixtus then drew together the five leading artists of the time—Sandro Botticelli, Perugino, Cosi-

it difficult to work out exactly which works he painted by himself.

But Botticelli's studio was not an especially serious place—there was time for fun too. Some people said that Botticelli only worked when he felt like it, and that his assistants were "idlers." Botticelli was known for enjoying playing practical jokes on his helpers. And the great 16th-century art historian of his contemporaries, Botticelli mostly painted religious works. Yet he is most famous for his paintings of mythological subjects—the stories of the gods and goddesses of ancient legend. He was the first Renaissance artist to paint mythologies with the seriousness traditionally reserved for religious themes. His classical goddesses are as grand and beautiful as his Madonnas.

A PRIVATE AUDIENCE

Botticelli painted mythological subjects for a different kind of audience from that of his religious pictures. Paintings of Christ and biblical stories had to

> "Sandro was an uncommonly good draftsman and ... his drawings ... show great skill and judgement." (Giorgio Vasari)

mo Rosselli, Domenico Ghirlandaio—who employed Michelangelo as an apprentice—and Luca Signorelli—to decorate the chapel with portraits of previous popes, and various scenes from the lives of Moses and Christ.

Botticelli painted three frescoes in the chapel during the summer of 1481, including *The Punishment of the Rebels*, an elaborate and detailed work.

Giorgio Vasari also notes that the artist "earned a great deal of money but wasted it all though carelessness and lack of management." Yet he also decribes the way in which Botticelli "threw himself into his work with diligence and enthusiasm."

By the standards of his time, Botticelli was a highly productive artist. He was also a versatile one. Like most

appeal to a wide public. But mythologies such as *Primavera* were intended for the private enjoyment of sophisticated, literary patrons. A patron would tell the painter exactly what he wanted in the picture. Therefore, these works often contained complex symbolism, making them hard to understand today.

With works such as *Primavera* and *Birth of Venus*, Botticelli brought new dignity to mythological painting, which

Primavera, c.1478, by Sandro Botticelli
Vasari described Botticelli's elegant mythological work as showing "Venus [goddess of love] as a symbol of spring being adorned with flowers by the Graces [the handmaidens of Venus]." Scholars have interpreted the painting in a variety of different ways.

was previously considered a minor form of artistic expression. Although the true meaning of these works is still debated today, their exquisite beauty has made them two of the most popular pictures ever painted.

AN ORIGINAL STYLE

Much of the beauty and elegance of these works lies in the most distinctive feature of Botticelli's style—its graceful linearity, or use of line. All his forms are clearly outlined, and he makes little use of light and shade to create an effect of three dimensions. Instead he concentrates on fluid and decorative designs— even if it means things look less

realistic. One 20th-century art critic described Botticelli as "The greatest artist of linear design that Europe has ever had."

CHANGE IN FLORENCE

By the 1490s, life was changing for Botticelli. Lorenzo de' Medici died in 1492. His son Piero took over, but he was a weak leader. Seizing this opportunity, Charles VIII of France invaded Italy. Although the city of Florence itself was spared attack, Piero surrendered various Florentine lands. He then fled the city, hounded out by its citizens.

In Piero's place, a highly zealous monk called Girolamo Savonarola became ruler. Savonarola had long been criticizing the corruption in Florence, and had also helped to prevent Charles from devastating the city.

A NEW INTENSITY

Botticelli soon became a follower of Savonarola. The artist was apparently a passionate admirer of the fanatical monk's sermons. His paintings changed, becoming more emotional and religious in their mood.

Savonarola's government came to an abrupt end, however. His many enemies succeeded in getting him cast out of the Church by the pope. He was put on trial for being a false prophet, and executed in 1498. His followers now had to hide away and meet in secret; this probably included Botticelli.

A FALL IN POPULARITY

Botticelli was now receiving fewer and fewer commissions. Many artists were producing paintings that looked very realistic and three-dimensional, and Botticelli's style appeared rather flat and old-fashioned alongside them.

This was made worse when Botticelli's great contemporary, Leonardo da Vinci, returned to Florence in 1500. The style Leonardo had been developing made the people in his pictures look more realistic than ever before, modeled out of subtle changes in light and shade. Yet that year, Botticelli painted the *Mystic Nativity*, which shows his indifference to the advances that artists had achieved during the 15th century.

By 1505, Botticelli had so little work that he was unable to pay fees to the artists' association to which he belonged. Some people still respected him, but his reputation was slipping. He could no longer stand up straight and had to use crutches to walk. He died in 1510, an "old and useless" man, according to Vasari.

After his death, visitors swarmed to the Sistine Chapel to see the work of the artists there—especially Michelangelo's (*see page 56*) ceiling, completed in 1512—but they walked straight past Botticelli's once-loved frescoes.

A NEW BEGINNING

Botticelli's work fell into obscurity and was still known by very few people as recently as the 19th century. Then, in the mid-1800s, two important British art critics, John Ruskin and Walter Pater, helped to restore his reputation, which has lasted to this day. At last, people saw that Botticelli's elegant figures and decorative style had a special beauty of their own.

MAJOR WORKS

1470	FORTITUDE
1475	THE ADORATION OF THE MAGI
c.1478	PRIMAVERA
c.1482	THE BIRTH OF VENUS
c.1480-85	MADONNA OF THE MAGNIFICAT
1489-90	THE ANNUNCIATION
1500	THE MYSTIC NATIVITY

HIERONYMUS BOSCH

The disturbing paintings of the Netherlandish artist Hieronymus Bosch have a strong moral message, which he communicated with great force by using a mixture of horribly vivid images and highly realistic details.

Hieronymus Bosch, whose full name was Jheronimous van Aeken, was born around 1450 in 's Hertogenbosch, a lively and wealthy town near Antwerp, in the Netherlands. Little is known of his childhood. The family may have come originally from Germany. The young man may have started to use the name Bosch—taken from his birthplace—when he went abroad. Another theory is that he used it as a way of distinguishing himself from his father, his sister, and one of his brothers, who were also painters.

AN ARTISTIC UPBRINGING

Bosch's family lived in a large house in the central square of the town, and the young man probably had a comfortable and settled early life. Artistic influences were all around him. He probably learned much of his craft in his father's studio, and he may have received further training in nearby Utrecht.

It is likely that there was a great emphasis on religious matters in the Bosch household. Religion was an important part of life in the Low Countries—modern Belgium, Luxembourg, and the Netherlands—at this time, and was especially important in the town of 's Hertogenbosch. All kinds of religious processions took place in the city, religious groups flourished, and there were many monasteries and convents, as well as the magnificent Cathedral of St. John.

A RELIGIOUS MAN

It would have been impossible for Bosch not to have been influenced by the intensely religious mood of his birthplace. He became involved with a zealous group called the Brethren of the Common Life. The Brethren believed that they lived in corrupt times, and that they needed to fight this by being spiritual and pure.

Engraving of Hieronymus Bosch, 17th century, after a contemporary artist
Little is known about this quirky line engraving of the artist.

During the late 1470s or early 1480s, Bosch married Aleyt Goyaerts van den Meervenne, who was quite a few years older than he was. She came from a noble family, and Bosch gained various lands and properties through the match.

Bosch's wife was responsible for making him even more religious. She was a member of a group called The Brotherhood of Our Lady. This group had great influence in the city. It organized both religious events and secular, or worldly, matters, which included the commissioning of paintings.

The Brotherhood kept detailed records of its activities; most of the little information we know about Bosch's life comes from these records. In 1486, the artist was accepted into the Brotherhood as a "sworn brother." This honor meant that he was generally considered to be an eminent and devout man.

A RISING REPUTATION

Bosch had already undertaken important commissions for religious paintings. Around 1490, he was painting the shutters for an altarpiece of Our Lady. The central section of this altarpiece had been carved by Adriaen van Wesel, a famous and well-respected sculptor.

At about the same time, Bosch painted *The Hay Wain*. This is regarded as the first painting in which he revealed his unique imagination. It is based on a Flemish proverb: "The world is a haystack, and everyone snatches what he can from it." The work is a triptych in format—a central panel with two wings which fold over it. The left wing is painted with the Garden of Eden. And

ST. JOHN'S CATHEDRAL

This magnificent cathedral in his hometown of 's Hertogenbosch played a central part in Bosch's life.

St. John's Cathedral was one of the finest buildings in Bosch's hometown. The building of the cathedral took a very long time; begun in the 1300s, it was not finished until the 1500s. The cathedral was a perfect expression of the wealth, confidence, and devotion of the people of 's Hertogenbosch.

Hertogenbosch was a city made rich by the cloth trade, yet which retained its medieval religious beliefs. There were countless religious groups in the city, and one of the most eminent, the Brotherhood of Our Lady, had a beautiful chapel there. When the Brotherhood

the right wing shows hell, a terrifying scene of smoke and flames, darkness, and bizarre details.

The bizarre scenes in Bosch's paintings can be difficult to understand today. But the public of his own time understood his fantastic creations as serious, highly moral tales. Yet however fabulous they appear, his subjects are rooted in what Bosch and his con-

decided to build a new chapel, in 1478, various members of the Bosch family were commissioned to help with painting, sculpture, and decoration.

Bosch himself designed stained glass, a crucifix, and a chandelier. He also painted two altarpieces, and various Old Testament scenes, which no longer exist.

temporaries considered to be reality—man's evil and sinful nature. One 16th-century collector described Bosch's subject matter as "the habits and passions of the soul of man."

In its content, Bosch's art is very different from most 15th-century Flemish painting. His contemporaries usually painted traditional, biblical themes. But Bosch delved far deeper

into the darker side of the human mind. He took his images from a wide variety of sources, from alchemy and magic, to witchcraft and astrology. He also drew on the proverbs and lively folklore of his day.

AN ORIGINAL STYLE

Bosch's style was also out of the mainstream. Most contemporary painters used a slow and painstaking technique in order to render forms as realistically as possible. But Bosch worked quickly—often without revision—to achieve his dreamlike effects. Yet he did not sacrifice detail; his work is very precise and carefully composed.

"If there are any absurdities here, they are ours, not his." (Fray José de Sigüenza on Bosch's paintings)

Bosch had a good drawing technique. This is clear from the drawings and sketches by him that have survived. He did these in ink using pen and brush. Many of the sketches show beggars, cripples, and monsters, and were intended as preparatory studies for his paintings. He created these lively drawings quickly and with vigor.

Bosch's works also display a strong sense of drama. Vigorous actions,

Christ Carrying the Cross, 1510-16, by Hieronymus Bosch
In the center of this swirling mass of ugly, evil faces is Christ bearing the cross to Golgotha, where he would be crucified. His calm face reflects his resignation to his fate.

exaggerated poses, and intense facial expressions—often in profile, or sideways on—characterize many of his paintings. The ugliness of his characters expresses their inner evil. Bosch was a master of the grotesque, and often used caricature, or comic distortion, to reveal man at his most wicked.

Bosch produced haunting tales of human sin that dared to tell what he saw as the full truth. Such scenes as *Christ Carrying the Cross* help to explain why one 16th-century poet described the content of the artist's terrifying visions as "Specters and apparitions of Hell."

People certainly recognized Bosch's vision and gift as unique. According to a Spanish priest of the 17th century, his uniqueness lay in the fact that, whereas other painters painted "man as he is on the outside," Bosch had the "audacity to paint him as he is on the inside."

But Bosch did not only paint visions of sin and punishment. He also painted beautiful landscapes that were to have an enormous influence on the artists who followed him.

Throughout his life, Bosch and his relatives undertook several jobs for the Brotherhood's chapel, in St. John's Cathedral. It was here that an image of the Virgin Mary was kept, which was rumored to possess the power to perform miracles. Around 1493, Bosch started to design a stained glass window for the chapel. There are stories that he planned his design on "a pair of old bedsheets."

EARTHLY DELIGHTS

Little is known about Bosch's life for the first few years of the 1500s. Some critics think that he may have been traveling in Italy at this time. Between 1500 to 1510, however, he painted his largest and most complex work, *The Garden of Earthly Delights*. Although the monsters in this three-paneled work are the most hideous Bosch ever created, the painting has extraordinary beauty and richness of color. As in *The Hay Wain*, the central panel represents humankind's sinful activities.

By 1504, Bosch appears back in the records of the Brotherhood once again. By now, he was a highly regarded artist.

This was the year that Philip the Fair, the Duke of Burgundy, who loved art, gave Bosch a major commission—to paint a huge altarpiece, of about 10-foot square, on the theme of the Last Judgment. On one side there was to be a scene of heaven, and on the other side a scene of hell.

This piece of work has never been found, although there are many theories surrounding it. We know something about what it would have looked like, however, since Bosch painted a smaller work on the same subject which is now in Vienna.

FINAL YEARS

In the later stages of his life, Bosch was undertaking regular work for the Brotherhood. This included producing designs for a crucifix and a chandelier, between 1511 and 1513. In 1516, the artist died in the city of his birth. Announcements of his death described him as an "illustrious painter."

MAJOR WORKS

c.1470-80	ECCE HOMO
1475-80	THE CURE OF FOLLY; THE SEVEN DEADLY SINS
c.1490	THE HAY WAIN; THE CROWNING OF THORNS
c.1500-10	THE GARDEN OF EARTHLY DELIGHTS; THE TEMPTATION OF ST. ANTHONY
1510-16	CHRIST CARRYING THE CROSS

LEONARDO DA VINCI

Perhaps the most versatile genius who ever lived, Leonardo reached the heights of human achievement. Not only one of the greatest painters of the Renaissance, he was also a talented scientist, designer, and musician.

Leonardo da Vinci was born on April 15, 1452, in or near the little town of Vinci, a day's journey from Florence, in central Italy. He was the illegitimate son of a lawyer and a peasant girl. Leonardo's father, Piero da Vinci, later married four times, and the boy eventually had 11 half brothers and sisters, all much younger than himself.

From 1466, Piero lived in Florence, where his legal career flourished. Leonardo entered the workshop of Andrea del Verrocchio, a famous artist in the city. Verrocchio was mainly a sculptor, but he was a painter too. Leonardo learned various artistic techniques from his master.

A PRECOCIOUS TALENT

In 1472, at the age of 20, Leonardo qualified as a master painter. But instead of setting up independently, he worked with Verrocchio for several more years. Giorgio Vasari, whose book of artists' lives was published in 1550, wrote that Leonardo's skill with the brush astounded Verrocchio so much that the teacher decided to give up painting for good.

In spite of his technical skill, however, Leonardo was always more interested in planning and thinking about art than in putting his ideas into action. Once he had finished working out a project, he tended to lose interest and not complete it. His brilliant mind would then start exploring some other problem. In one case, he took 25 years to complete a commission because he got so distracted with other projects.

Leonardo stayed in Florence until 1481 or 1482, when he moved north to Milan. There, he hoped to find work at the court of Duke Ludovico Sforza, the ruler of the city. Ludovico was an art lover, but first and foremost he was a soldier. Leonardo wrote him a letter offering his services as a designer of

Self-portrait, c.1512, by Leonardo da Vinci
Leonardo drew this delicate image of himself when he was around 60 years old.

instruments of war. He mentioned his artistic skills almost as an afterthought.

Leonardo's letter had the desired effect, and he received a commission from Ludovico to produce an enormous statue of the duke's father, Francesco, on horseback. Leonardo only got as far as making a full-scale clay model of the horse, however. The statue was so large that he could never assemble the 90-odd tons of bronze required for its casting.

His other great undertaking in Milan was a wall painting of *The Last Supper* for the monastery of Santa Maria delle Grazie, which he painted in around 1495. Its brilliance was indisputable and even before Leonardo had finished the work, it drew many admiring pilgrims.

The artist had used an experimental technique that proved disastrous, however. Instead of using the normal kind of paint for painting on wet plaster—a technique known as fresco— Leonardo had chosen a paint for use on wood. Within a few years, the picture was peeling off the wall. At the time of the painting's completion, no one knew that it would deteriorate so quickly, and it became the most revered painting in the world.

At the age of 42, Leonardo was at the peak of his career, admired and respected by all. Around this time, he began to write his *Treatise on Painting,* which he never finished.

MASTER OF INVENTION

In addition to his artistic work, Leonardo immersed himself in scientific research. He filled several notebooks with sketches and comments written in

THE LAST SUPPER

Leonardo's vision of Jesus' final meal with the disciples was his best-known work while he was alive.

Leonardo painted his famous wall painting, *The Last Supper*, in the refectory—or dining-room— of the monastery of Santa Maria delle Grazie, Milan (*right*), in around 1495. The subject was an appropriate one for a refectory, for it represented the most famous meal in the Bible. The painting covered one of the end walls of the room. The monks would look at it as they ate their meals and think deeply about its important story.

The picture shows the moment when Jesus Christ shocks his disciples by saying that one of them will betray him. Leonardo worked on it in his

mirror-image writing. Some people think he used this script to keep his discoveries secret, but perhaps it was just easier for him to write that way— across the page from right to left— because he was left-handed. He found the humblest subjects worthy of study: birds, plants, the movement of water. Above all, he was fascinated by human anatomy and dissected over 30 bodies.

variety of fields won him widespread acclaim throughout Europe.

In 1499, a French army invaded Milan and Duke Ludovico lost control of the city. Leonardo headed south. He soon found new work, not as an artist, however, but as a military engineer for Cesare Borgia, one of the most famous soldiers of the time, who was engaged in warfare in central Italy.

GREAT WORKS

After his work for Borgia, Leonardo returned to Florence. In 1504, he received a great commission from the city to paint *The Battle of Anghiari*. This was to glorify an encounter in a war some 60 years earlier between the Florentine republic and Milan, its main rival city-state. It gave Leonardo an opportunity to show his skill at painting horses and depicting movement—two areas in which he was unrivaled. Leonardo used the same experimental technique as he had with *The Last Supper*. The picture deteriorated so badly that it was later painted over.

From Leonardo's own drawings and from copies of the painting, it is possible to get some idea of what the magnificent work looked like. It showed men and horses in deadly combat. No other artist had succeeded so well in conveying what Leonardo called the "bestial madness" of war.

At around the same time as he was working on *The Battle of Anghiari*, Leonardo painted his most famous work, the *Mona Lisa*, a portrait of Lisa Gherardini. She was the wife of Francesco del Giocondo, a Florentine

customary slow and thoughtful way. He tried to find exactly the right poses and expressions to depict the drama and human emotion of the situation. At one point, the prior of the monastery is said to have urged the painter to work more quickly. Leonardo replied that he was having difficulty finding a suitably treacherous face to represent Judas—the disciple who be-trayed Jesus—but if speed was essential, he would use the prior's face as a model.

Leonardo also produced designs for several ingenious machines, including a submarine and a tank. The most ambitious of these was a helicopter. Leonardo's plan for a flying machine was unsuccessful, however: He had no suitable source of power. Human muscles were simply not strong enough to get his contraption in the air. Nonetheless, his astonishing skill in a

Mona Lisa, c.1503, by Leonardo da Vinci
**This picture is famous for its subject's strange, enchanting smile. It is
thought Leonardo used jesters to keep "Mona" Lisa amused as he worked.**

merchant. Because of this, the painting
is also known as *La Giaconda*.

The portrait is now so familiar that
it is hard to appreciate how original the
pose and expression were in their
naturalism and subtlety. No other artist
had ever blended light and shade so
delicately to depict human forms. This
technique was called *sfumato*, from the
Italian word *fumo*, meaning smoke.

Leonardo blended his tones so smoothly that they merged, in his own words, "without lines or borders in the manner of smoke." Many artists were influenced by this aspect of Leonardo's

---

"Leonardo's name and fame will never be extinguished...." (Giorgio Vasari)

---

work. The large number of copies of his paintings shows the tremendous influence he had on others.

INCOMPLETE PROJECTS

By 1506, Leonardo was back in Milan, this time working for the French. He planned another huge statue. Ironically, this one was of Gian Giacomo Trivulzio, the Italian general who had led the French army that drove Leonardo's former employer, Ludovico Sforza, out of Milan. Leonardo never completed the statue, however.

In 1512, the Sforza family once more seized control of Milan. Because of his involvement with the French, Leonardo decided it was wise to move elsewhere. He went to Rome, hoping to work for the pope. Leonardo was now 60, however, and many patrons were reluctant to employ him because they thought he was too old and unreliable.

In any case, there were already two artistic giants in Rome, Michelangelo and Raphael (see pages 56 and 62). These were younger men who had already proved they could carry daunting projects through to a triumphant conclusion. Michelangelo had just completed his mammoth task of decorating the ceiling of the Sistine Chapel. Although Leonardo was treated with respect in Rome, he received no commissions. With little hope of finding work in Italy, he accepted an offer from the art-loving King Francis I of France, to move to his country.

LAST DAYS IN FRANCE

In 1516, Leonardo settled in a manor house provided by the king in the Loire Valley, near the royal palace of Amboise. He was no longer strong, and his left hand was partly paralyzed. He made designs for court entertainments, planned architectural projects, and prepared his notebooks for publication. He died peacefully at Amboise on May 2, 1519, shortly after his 67th birthday.

MAJOR WORKS

c.1472	THE ANNUNCIATION
c.1474	GINEVRA DE' BENCI
c.1485	LADY WITH AN ERMINE
c.1495-97	THE LAST SUPPER
c.1499	VIRGIN AND CHILD WITH ST. ANNE AND JOHN THE BAPTIST
c.1503	MONA LISA
c.1508	THE VIRGIN OF THE ROCKS

ALBRECHT DÜRER

One of the most important figures of the northern Renaissance, Dürer brought the achievements of Italian art to his native Germany. His detailed prints established his reputation throughout Europe.

Albrecht Dürer was born on May 21, 1471, in Nuremberg, a city in southern Germany. He was the son of a goldsmith and the third child in a family of 18. As was the custom, Albrecht learned his father's craft. But his preference for painting was soon apparent, much to his father's dismay.

In 1486, at the age of 15, he began a three-year apprenticeship in the workshop of Michael Wolgemut, a local artist and printmaker. A print is an image made from an inked impression of an engraved metal plate or wooden block.

YOUNG MAN'S TRAVELS

In 1490, Dürer set off on the traditional "bachelor's year," a period when a young man could see the world before settling down to family life. Dürer's travels, in fact, lasted almost four years. He visited many parts of France, Switzerland, and Germany.

Dürer returned to Nuremberg in 1494, and married Agnes Frey, the daughter of a local coppersmith. Little is known about the marriage, but it seems to have been one of convenience rather than of affection. They had no children and a friend of Dürer's described Agnes as "nagging, shrewish, and greedy."

ITALIAN INFLUENCE

Soon after his marriage, Dürer set off again on his travels, this time to the north Italian city of Venice. For an artist, it was an exciting time to visit Italy. The recent advances made by Italian painters and sculptors had revolutionized art. Dürer had much to learn. He copied the works of the Italian masters and studied ideas about proportion and perspective, the new method of showing depth in a picture.

Dürer liked the way Italians respected their artists and treated them like celebrities. In Germany, people thought artists were merely craftsmen.

Self-portrait, 1498, by Albrecht Dürer
Dürer was proud of his appearance and painted several self-portraits. Here, he shows himself wearing elegant clothes.

1498.

Das malt ich nach meiner gestalt
Ich war sex und zwenzig Jor alt
Albrecht Dürer

The Knight, Death, and the Devil, 1513, by Albrecht Dürer
This engraving reveals Dürer's skill at showing fine detail. The knight represents the Christian faith. His strength and courage take him past the powers of darkness.

Dürer complained: "In Italy I am a gentleman, at home a parasite."

Dürer returned home in 1495. He was determined to bring the achievements of the Italian artists to German soil. His emphasis on the human figure and his concern with ideal beauty and proportion were typically Italian. Like Leonardo da Vinci (*see page 46*), Dürer was also fascinated by the natural world and produced several detailed paintings of plants and animals.

As well as paintings, Dürer also made a large number of prints. The striking feature of these was his mastery of the tiniest detail, a difficult feat in print-making. One of Dürer's first major works was a series of illustrations called *The Apocalypse.* These were printed at the press of his godfather, Anton Koberger, but Dürer insisted that his own name appear as the publisher. This was typical of his strong character, and of his determination to raise the status of the artist in Germany.

Over the next few years, Dürer worked hard and became one of Nuremberg's leading artists. His mother and wife sold his prints at the town's markets. Often, traveling merchants would buy them and take them abroad.

By 1505, Dürer's prints were well known all over Europe. That year, he made another visit to Italy. In Venice, he received a commission to paint an altarpiece for the wealthy German merchant community. All who saw the finished work praised Dürer's genius. Many eminent people came to see him in his studio.

After he returned to Nuremberg in 1507, Dürer's career went from strength to strength. From 1512 onward, he worked for the Holy Roman Emperor, Maximilian I, who ruled over much of northern Europe. In recognition of Dürer's skill, Maximilian awarded the artist a generous annual pension.

In spite of his success, however, Dürer had problems. His mother died in 1514, an event which upset him greatly.

Shortly after this, he underwent a spiritual crisis. European religion as a whole was in upheaval. In 1517, the German priest Martin Luther launched a crusade for reform of the Roman Catholic Church. Luther's campaign ultimately led to the Reformation—the Protestant revolution against the Church. Dürer read Luther's writings closely and became a passionate believer in the Protestant cause.

TRIUMPHANT JOURNEY

In 1519, Maximilian died, and Dürer's pension came to an end. He had to travel to the Netherlands to ask the new emperor, Charles V, to renew his allowance. On his journey, Dürer visited many parts of the Netherlands. Now, everywhere he went he was celebrated as the greatest German artist of the age.

Dürer returned to Nuremberg in 1521. In his final years, he lived quietly, concentrating on studying and writing books on art theory. He died in Nuremberg on April 6, 1528, at the age of 57.

MAJOR WORKS

1498	THE FOUR HORSEMEN OF THE APOCALYPSE
1502	A HARE
1504	THE FALL OF MAN; ADORATION OF THE MAGI
1513	THE KNIGHT, DEATH, AND THE DEVIL
1514	MELENCOLIA I
1526	THE FOUR APOSTLES

MICHELANGELO BUONARROTI

One of the greatest figures in the history of art, Michelangelo was not only an astonishingly talented sculptor, but also a painter, poet, and architect. Even during his own lifetime, he was called "divine."

Michelangelo was born on March 6, 1475, in the small town of Caprese, near Arezzo in northern Italy. Michelangelo's father was the town mayor. When his term of office ended, he returned to his native Florence, where Michelangelo grew up.

Michelangelo was determined to be an artist. But his father disapproved of his artistic ambition. The Buonarroti family claimed to have aristocratic blood, and it was not considered fitting for a gentleman to work with his hands. Painters and sculptors were regarded as mere craftsmen.

EARLY PROMISE
In spite of his father's opposition, Michelangelo began training with the Florentine artist Domenico Ghirlandaio in 1488, when he was 13. Although he must have learned the basics of painting techniques here, Michelangelo thought of himself as essentially self-taught.

After about a year with Ghirlandaio, Michelangelo was already singled out as an exceptionally talented boy. He went to work in an informal academy held in gardens belonging to the Medici family, who were virtually the rulers of Florence. Michelangelo studied works of ancient sculpture that were displayed in the gardens, and soon began to carve stone statues.

He created his earliest surviving sculptures when he was about 16 years old. These works show remarkable technical skill for his age. Although he occasionally worked in wood or bronze, the material that he loved was marble.

In 1492, the head of the Medici family, Lorenzo, died, and the government of Florence became less stable. Two years later, Michelangelo moved to Bologna, in northern Italy, and then, after a brief return to Florence, he went to Rome, now the country's capital, in 1496. He remained there for five years.

David (detail), 1501-04, by Michelangelo **Few portraits of the artist exist. This sculpture shows the biblical hero, David, just before he kills the giant, Goliath.**

skill at capturing a sitter's expression and personality. As an art critic wrote some 30 years after the painter's death, "Raphael painted figures of every sort, some delicate, some fearsome, and some vigorous."

Raphael revealed his talent in his work for Pope Julius' successor, Leo X. His portrait of Leo with two cardinals, painted in 1518, is one of Raphael's finest. The exquisite rendering of the clothes, facial expressions, and objects inspired great admiration; Vasari even commented that it was "more lifelike than life itself."

As well as working for the pope and other important figures in the Church, Raphael also carried out commissions for other patrons. These included Agostino Chigi, a wealthy banker. Raphael designed a wall decoration for Chigi's palatial villa just outside the walls of Rome—the Villa Farnesina.

Raphael worked in a very careful and painstaking way. He made drawings for every stage of his compositions. These included sketches of heads and hands, detailed drapery studies, and preliminary studies of groups of figures. Yet despite this methodical approach, his works reveal nothing of their elaborate planning, and always keep a sense of naturalness and spontaneity.

ROMAN ARCHITECT

Raphael also designed buildings. In 1514, he was made architect to the church of St. Peter's, which stands close to the Vatican in Rome. As with everything he did, Raphael was a success as an architect. Most of his work in this field has since been altered or destroyed, however.

Raphael's style as an architect was influenced by the grand buildings of ancient Rome, which he studied very closely. Indeed, in 1519, he began a survey of all the ancient remains in the city, but never completed it.

In the spring of 1520, Raphael got sick. He died on April 6 that year. It is likely that he contracted a simple fever. At his own request, Raphael was buried in the Pantheon, the only building from the time of the Roman Empire to have survived more or less intact.

LASTING REPUTATION

The great fame that Raphael enjoyed in his lifetime became even greater after his death. For centuries, no one could match Raphael's range, variety, and grace. And today, despite a brief loss of popularity during the 19th century, Raphael continues to be regarded as one of the greatest painters of all time.

MAJOR WORKS

1504	THE BETROTHAL OF THE VIRGIN
c.1506	MADONNA DEL GRANDUCA
1507	THE MADONNA OF THE GOLDFINCH; THE ENTOMBMENT
1509-11	THE SCHOOL OF ATHENS
1513-14	THE LIBERATION OF ST. PETER; SISTINE MADONNA
1517-20	THE TRANSFIGURATION

TITIAN

For more than 50 years, Titian was the leading painter in Venice, northern Italy. He was Europe's leading portrait painter, and was also famous for his religious works and scenes from ancient mythology.

Titian was born Tiziano Vecellio, in Pieve di Cadore, a small town in the Italian Alps ruled by the republic of Venice. His father was a town official.

There is no record of Titian's birthdate, but most scholars think he was born in around 1485. Little is known about Titian's life until about 1510—except that he trained in the studio of Giovanni Bellini, the outstanding Venetian painter of his generation.

AN EARLY INFLUENCE

Bellini probably also taught another gifted young painter, Giorgione. Titian and Giorgione worked closely together. In 1508, they collaborated on some frescoes that attracted great praise.

After Giorgione's death in 1510, Titian apparently completed several of his colleague's paintings. He imitated Giorgione's dreamy and romantic style so closely that it is sometimes difficult to tell their work apart.

In 1511, another rising Venetian painter, Sebastiano del Piombo, moved to Rome, leaving Titian as the leading young painter in Venice. When Giovanni Bellini died in 1516, Titian succeeded him as Venice's official painter.

He proved his ability by painting a huge altarpiece for Santa Maria dei Frari, one of the most important churches in Venice, between 1516 and 1518. Its subject, *The Assumption of the Virgin*, shows the moment when Jesus' mother, the Virgin Mary, is taken up into heaven. Titian's version of the scene shows Mary being lifted on a cloud, in a glorious burst of color and movement. By now, Titian had left Giorgione's poetic style behind for something much stronger and more powerful.

IMPORTANT CONTACT

Around this time, he received an invitation from Alfonso d'Este, duke of Ferrara, northern Italy, who became

Self-portrait, c.1576, by Titian
This somber self-portrait dates from the year that the artist died, probably when he was around 90 years old.

one of his most important patrons. Through him, Titian met the rulers of other Italian cities who prided themselves on their learning. Among other commissions, Titian began a series of mythological paintings for Alfonso's study. These included *Bacchus and Ariadne* and *The Andrians*, two of his best-known works.

Titian's fame spread rapidly, and he was soon regarded as the best painter in Italy. The other great painters of the time were either dead—Leonardo da Vinci (*see page 46*) had died in 1519, and Raphael (*see page 62*) in 1520—or working in other art forms, like Michelangelo (*see page 56*), who now worked as a sculptor and architect.

Titian enjoyed his success. In 1531, he moved into a large house on the eastern edge of Venice, with gardens overlooking the lagoon, where he gave visitors a lavish welcome. Some of his closest friends were among Venice's most important citizens. Titian's wife, Cornelia, had died in 1530, leaving their children to be brought up by her sister, Orsola, who looked after the painter's household until her death in 1550.

A GREAT HONOR

In 1530, Titian was in Bologna, in northern Italy, where he met the king of Spain, Charles V, who had been elected Holy Roman Emperor in 1519. At first, Titian did not impress the powerful ruler. But within the next few years, he had become the emperor's favorite painter, as well as a close friend.

In 1533, Charles made Titian a Count Palatine and Knight of the Golden

TITIAN'S MYTHOLOGIES

Aristocrats who wanted to display their education commissioned paintings of Greek and Roman legends.

For centuries, religious subjects had dominated art. But Titian lived at a time when scenes from ancient history, myths, and legends were becoming very popular themes for painters, especially those working for learned patrons.

The popularity of scenes from ancient Greek and Roman myths was part of the rediscovery of the civilization of the ancient world that took place during the Renaissance. In the 1470s, the painter Sandro Botticelli (*see page 34*) had been one of the first artists to paint mythological subjects in a serious way, and on a big scale.

Spur—a position which had all the privileges of knighthood and nobility. It was the first time that a painter had been awarded such high honors. Charles tried to persuade Titian to visit Spain to paint portraits of the royal family there, but the artist refused.

Titian painted the emperor several times. These works reveal the great range and variety he brought to portrai-

One of Titian's most famous mythological works is *Bacchus and Ariadne* (above), which he painted for Alfonso d'Este, The picture illustrates a story written by the Roman poets Ovid and Catullus. The exuberant scene shows the wine god, Bacchus, and his followers coming across Ariadne, daughter of King Minos of Crete, who has been abandoned by her lover, Theseus. Titian captures the moment when Bacchus sees Ariadne for the first time, and instantly falls in love with her.

also introduced accessories, such as a dog or a musical instrument, into his portraits. These helped him to vary the picture's composition—the arrangement of figures and objects within the picture. The extra items also suggested the interests or status of the sitter. For generations afterward, portrait painters adopted Titian's poses and ideas.

IN DEMAND

During the late 1540s, Titian overcame his reluctance to travel, visiting Rome between 1545 and 1546 as the guest of

> "I believe that a blotch by Titian will be better than anything by another artist."
> (16th-century Spanish nobleman)

Pope Paul III, whose portrait he painted. In 1548, the artist crossed the Alps to work for nine months at Charles V's court at Augsburg, western Germany.

On the way back from Germany, Titian met Charles V's son, Philip II of Spain, in Milan. Philip also grew to admire the Venetian's work, and became the most important patron of Titian's later career.

Philip was intensely devout, and Titian's work for him included religious pictures as well as portraits. But the most impressive pictures Titian painted

ture. Up until the early 16th century, most portraits showed only the head and shoulders of the person in the picture. While Titian was not the first artist to paint portraits showing the whole body, he helped make this type of portrait very popular.

His portraits of Charles show the emperor in a variety of poses—standing, seated, and on horseback. Titian

Noli me Tangere, c.1508, by Titian
This early painting tells the story of Christ's appearance to Mary Magdalen after the Resurrection. Mary reached out to Christ but he said, "Touch me not"—"Noli me tangere."

for him are a series depicting erotic scenes from classical mythology, which he worked on between 1550 and 1562.

Philip and Titian wrote to each other frequently concerning these and other works. The letters show the artist in an unattractive light, for he was constantly asking for money. Admittedly, the king often took a long time to pay the painter. But Titian claimed he was living in poverty, which was non-sense. He even exaggerated his age to try to gain sympathy from Philip; this is one reason why no one is sure of his true birthdate.

By this time, Titian was old. His sight started to fail, and he had increasing difficulty painting. He ran a large studio,

---

> "Titian ... deserves the love and respect of all craftsmen."
> (Giorgio Vasari)

---

and his assistants—including his brother, his cousin, and his son Orazio —carried out much of the work in some of his late paintings.

LATE TECHNIQUE
In his late works, Titian used oil paint in an open and expressive way. He delighted in the thick texture of the paint. The strokes of the brush were very loose—almost casual. According to one of Titian's last assistants, toward the end of his life, the artist painted more with his fingers than his brushes. He went beyond representing exact details and objects, and used paint to capture atmosphere and mood.

This technique helped Titian create pictures that were more inward-looking, and filled with religious feeling. His final painting was a deeply moving portrayal of the *Pietà*—the Virgin Mary holding the limp body of Jesus after the crucifixion. He intended this to be hung over his own tomb in his burial chapel. In this work he depicted himself as St. Jerome gazing reverently into Jesus' lifeless face.

VIEWING THE CANVAS
Many people did not appreciate Titian's way of painting. When Philip II first saw his *Portrait in Armor* of around 1550, for example, he declared: "It is easy to see the haste with which it has been painted, and if there had been more time I would have had him do it over again." But, as Philip's aunt, Queen Mary of England, realized, some of Titian's paintings need to be viewed from a distance. If the viewer goes too close to the canvas, the picture dissolves into a series of smudges.

When Titian died in Venice on August 27, 1576, he was probably around 90 years old. He was buried in the church of Santa Maria Gloriosa dei Frari.

MAJOR WORKS

c.1514	SACRED AND PROFANE LOVE
1516-18	THE ASSUMPTION OF THE VIRGIN
c.1520-23	BACCHUS AND ARIADNE
1538	VENUS OF URBINO
1548	CHARLES V ON HORSEBACK
c.1549-50	DANAË

PIETER BRUEGHEL

Brueghel is famous for his lively, colorful, and humorous paintings of ordinary people going about their everyday lives. Yet while they seem lighthearted, these works contain serious moral messages.

Very little information exists about the life of this famous painter. It seems likely, however, that Pieter Brueghel the Elder, sometimes called "Peasant" Brueghel, was born between 1525 and 1530, in or near the city of Breda, in the province of Brabant, in the Netherlands. Today, the Netherlands is also sometimes called Holland.

LEARNING HIS TRADE

The few contemporary records that survive show that Brueghel became a master in the painter's guild—a trade association for artists—in Antwerp, in the north of modern Belgium, in 1551. At this time a major port, Antwerp was one of the richest cities in the world. Brueghel learned his trade as a pupil of Pieter Coecke van Aelst, working in his busy, successful workshop.

Van Aelst was interested in Italian painting, and this may have inspired Brueghel to set off on a tour of Italy, in 1552. At this time, Italy was a magnet that drew artists from all over Europe.

Brueghel traveled around the country, and visited Sicily, an island in the Mediterranean off the southern tip of Italy, and Naples, southern Italy. While he was in Italy, Brueghel probably worked in the Rome studio of Giulio Clovio, who specialized in decorative miniature paintings. The Dutch artist probably painted the landscapes, and the Italian painter added the figures.

INSPIRED BY THE ALPS

Although Brueghel enjoyed the Italian scenery, it was his passage across the Alps that most overwhelmed him. These great mountains were unlike anything that the young painter had seen in his own flat homeland. The grandeur of the mountains fired his imagination, and after he returned home, Brueghel's paintings often contained rocky landscapes.

The Artist and the Connoisseur (detail), 1566-68, by Pieter Brueghel
This pen and ink drawing is a presumed self-portrait of the artist at work.

By 1553, the artist was back home in Antwerp, working for Hieronymus Cock, a print publisher. A print is a work of art that exists in multiple copies. Publishers like Cock would make these images available to the public.

Brueghel's job was to produce engravings of landscape scenes. Engraving is a method of making prints, by cutting lines or dots into a hard surface. When the design is reproduced by printing on paper, the picture is called an engraving, or print. Artists made engravings of existing paintings, as well as inventing original works of art.

INFLUENCED BY BOSCH

Cock had a strong influence on Brueghel's work. He saw that his employee's style had some similarities to paintings by the Flemish artist, Hieronymus Bosch (*see page 40*), whose strange, disturbing images were becoming popular again. Cock asked Brueghel to make copies of the paintings, and then sold them, pretending they were originals.

Brueghel's paintings from this time, such as *The Netherlandish Proverbs* (1559), have a distinctive style. Lots of tiny figures are crammed into a busy scene, which shows all kinds of colorful details of village life. Every tiny scene in the painting tells its own story. Each one depicts a proverb and also highlights the foolishness of human ways. This style was common in popular prints of the time.

In 1563, the artist married Mayken, the daughter of his former employer, Pieter Coecke van Aelst, and settled in

A MORAL MESSAGE

Part of Brueghel's great talent lay in delivering messages in an interesting and stimulating way.

Although he is called "Peasant" Brueghel, because of his paintings of country life and ordinary local people (*right*), the artist was actually a sophisticated man of great learning. Under the surface of his lighthearted pictures lay moral messages about the issues of the day.

Many 16th-century artists tried to convey moral messages in their work. These were usually based on the teachings of the Christian church. Brueghel's messages were not so religious. He preferred instead to discuss people's weaknesses.

In his painting *The Netherlandish Proverbs*, Brueghel used

Brussels. At around 19 years old, Mayken was half Brueghel's age. The couple had two sons. Both of them, Jan the Elder and Pieter the Younger, became well-known artists.

Brussels was very different from Antwerp. While Antwerp was a flourishing center for trade, Brussels was a more cultural, aristocratic place. This was where Philip II of Spain, the head

famous Dutch sayings to show the folly of humankind. His mythological and biblical paintings, such as *The Fall of Icarus* and *The Parable of the Blind*, also teach a moral lesson.

The theme of blindness recurs in Brueghel's work. He continually highlights those who are blind to the stupidity of their actions. He also illustrates people being blind to the Church, and indulging in sins, such as gluttony or greed.

of the Holy Roman Empire, had his administrative headquarters. Philip had inherited the rule of the Netherlands from his father, Charles V, in 1556.

CHANGING STYLE

Brueghel found his new surroundings both exciting and stimulating, and soon found many rich patrons. His style became more sophisticated, too. In-

stead of scenes packed with people, Brueghel began to concentrate on just one subject. His figures also became larger and more realistic.

Brueghel produced a series of drawings from life during this period. These studies of peasants, soldiers, and tradesmen are carefully finished in chalk and pen and ink. Their detail suggests Brueghel finished them in the studio. Even so, they demonstrate that Brueghel was taking a direct interest in human subjects, rather than just working from sources such as the Bible, legends, and the classics.

Brueghel's biographer, Karl van Mander, recorded how Brueghel and a

> ## "He swallowed all the mountains and spat them out again ... on his canvases ...."
> ## (Van Mander on Brueghel in the Alps)

friend used to disguise themselves as peasants, and steal into the countryside to observe rustic weddings and fairs unseen. This story may not be true, but it was probably suggested by the artist's lively drawings and sketches.

During the 1560s, Brueghel also regained his enthusiasm for landscape. In 1565, a wealthy patron commissioned a series of six paintings showing the different months of the year. The five

Hunters in the Snow, 1565, by Pieter Brueghel
This bleak winter landscape, from Brueghel's series depicting the months of the year, probably depicts the month of January. It has a dramatic sense of space and depth.

that still exist, including *Hunters in the Snow*, are among Brueghel's best-loved works. No one had painted a landscape with such a sense of space and depth before. Landscape painting in northern Europe would never be the same again.

TROUBLED TIMES

Political troubles threw a cloud over the artist's final years. In the late 1560s, the people of the Netherlands revolted against Spanish rule. Brueghel felt torn. His patrons were the wealthy ruling lords—yet he loved his people and hated the prospect of war. Brueghel's paintings from this time reveal his unhappiness: Their mood is pessimistic and dark.

His final works were on a grander, more tragic scale; the humor of his early scenes has disappeared completely. Brueghel's later works mix realistic story-telling with a clear message, and set a distinctive style for the Dutch painters that followed him. Brueghel died in 1569, and, after his death, his reputation increased still further.

MAJOR WORKS

c.1558-66	THE FALL OF ICARUS
1559	NETHERLANDISH PROVERBS
1565	THE MONTHS
1568	THE PARABLE OF THE BLIND; THE WEDDING FEAST; THE PEASANT DANCE; THE MISANTHROPE

DANTE ALIGHIERI

Dante helped to create a literary Renaissance, or rebirth, with his masterpiece *The Divine Comedy*, which he wrote in Italian rather than the traditional Latin. He had a great impact on the world's writing for almost seven centuries.

Dante Alighieri was born in May 1265, in Florence, central Italy. His family had once been wealthy, but had fallen on hard times. Dante's father was a small businessman of some sort, possibly a moneylender. His mother died when he was about five, and his father later remarried and had other children. Dante had at least one half brother, Francesco, and one half sister, Tana. At school, Dante gained a good education in Latin literature.

A PURE LOVE

At the age of nine, Dante met the inspiration of his life: Bice Portinari, a beautiful eight-year-old girl. Beatrice, as he always called her, seemed perfect to the young Dante, and he would be obsessed with her all his life.

They did not know each other well— Dante only met her once again, in 1283, when she was 17, and she married another man. Dante, too, married another—Gemma Donati, in 1285— but Beatrice remained his inspiration.

With Gemma, Dante had four children: Giovanni, Pietro, Jacopo, and Antonia.

Beatrice died in 1290, aged just 24. Two years later, Dante wrote *The New Life*—a series of poems about Beatrice, accompanied by prose sections that describe the poet's meetings with her. Throughout the work, the poet remains devoted to Beatrice, and the poem ends with a vision of her at God's side. *The New Life* created the taste for a new type of poetry written out of love for an idealized woman.

POLITICAL PASSION

For five years after Beatrice's death, Dante was in the grip of grief. He tried to distract himself by throwing himself into the study of philosophy, theology, and the sciences.

In 1295, he became involved in the political life of Florence. There were

Dante inspires the city of Florence with his book The Divine Comedy *(detail), 1465, by Domenico di Michelino* **The poet stands outside his native city.**

two factions in the city: the Guelphs, who tended to support the pope, and the Ghibellines, who wanted imperial rule—by the Holy Roman Emperor, Frederick I. The Guelphs had won control of Florence in 1289, in the Battle of Campaldino. Dante himself was a Guelph, and had fought in that battle.

After they came to power, however, the Guelphs themselves split into two factions—the "Whites" and the "Blacks." Dante sided with the Whites, who were opposed to Pope Boniface VIII's attempts to interfere in Florence. They were also opposed to the Holy Roman Empire.

TRAVELING TO ROME

In 1301, Dante went to Rome with two other men to try to persuade the pope not to bring in a French prince, Charles of Valois, to settle the quarrels in Florence. They were unsuccessful.

While Dante was in Rome, Charles and his army helped the Blacks seize power from the Whites in Florence. In his absence, Dante was convicted of financial offenses, and of being an enemy of the pope. He was fined and banned from Florence for two years. When he did not report to the Blacks, or pay the fine, a heavier sentence was imposed—he would be burned alive if he was ever caught in Florence.

Dante loved his hometown. Being forced into exile was a devastating blow that cast a shadow over the rest of his career. In the next few years, he moved around Italy a good deal, probably settling for short periods at Padua, Ravenna, and Verona, in the northeast.

All this time, he was hard at work writing poetry and philosophy. In about 1305, he wrote *De Vulgari Eloquentia*, a pamphlet arguing that writers should use everyday Italian rather than Latin, since it was just as rich and vibrant a language. Ironically, however, Dante wrote this pamphlet in Latin, since it was intended for a learned audience. Before printing was introduced in the 15th century, nearly all manuscripts were written in Latin. It was an international language of learning.

In 1310, Dante wrote a political work, *Concerning Monarchy*, also in Latin. This proposed that kings and other political leaders should agree to be subject to a "universal emperor," who could impose solutions in disputes and see that justice was done.

THE DIVINE COMEDY

In about 1307, Dante began an epic poem, which he continued working on until his death 14 years later. He named it his *Comedy*, which he defined as a tale that begins sadly but has a happy ending. It was first printed in 1472. In 1555, it was published as *The Divine Comedy*, and has been known by this name ever since.

Dante's masterpiece was revolutionary. For Dante wrote his masterpiece not in formal Latin—but in Italian. The poem describes what happens to the souls of people after death. The Roman Catholic Church taught that the soul travels through the landscape of life after death. Hell is where sinners are sent, heaven is where the just and the good go, and purgatory is the place where those guilty of minor sins must prove that they are worthy of admission to heaven.

At the start of Dante's three-part poem, the narrator is lost in a forest roamed by wild animals. Then the Roman poet Virgil—author of the epic poem, the *Aeneid*—appears and offers to act as a guide.

In the first part, the poet and Virgil travel to Hell, where they witness the endless suffering of people who have been damned by God. In the second part, they visit Purgatory, a great mountain on whose sides famous figures from mythology and history must make up for the wicked things they did when alive on earth.

The travelers approach the summit of the mountain, a paradise on earth. Dante's inspiration, Beatrice, appears and Virgil leaves the poet in her care. In the third part, Dante and Beatrice travel through a beautiful land to the heavens, where the souls of the elect— the chosen ones—live with God.

A NEW FORM

Dante took great care with the form of the poem. He developed a complex pattern known as *terza rima*, in which the second line of each three-line verse rhymes with the first and third lines of the next verse. The first two parts are each divided into 33 cantos, or divisions, and the last has 34, making 100 cantos in total. The first part also has an introductory section.

In 1315, when he was in Verona, Dante was offered an opportunity to return to Florence. This offer was on condition that he admit that he was guilty of the crimes of which he had been accused, and go back as a penitent—a wrongdoer begging forgiveness. It was too much to ask, and the poet refused.

> "Midway through this way of life we're bound upon / I woke to find myself in a dark wood, / Where the right road was wholly lost and gone." (*The Divine Comedy*)

Shortly afterward, Dante settled in Ravenna, northeast of Florence. His family may have joined him there. On September 13, 1321, Dante died in Ravenna. He was buried with great ceremony in a chapel close to the church of San Francesco.

MAJOR WORKS

c.1292	THE NEW LIFE
c.1305	THE BANQUET; DE VULGARI ELOQUENTIA (ON ELOQUENCE IN THE COMMON TONGUE)
c.1307-21	THE DIVINE COMEDY
c.1310	CONCERNING MONARCHY

GEOFFREY CHAUCER

As well as being a scholar, courtier, and diplomat, Geoffrey Chaucer was also the father of English poetry. Although living in the Middle Ages, his use of everyday language places him within the Renaissance spirit.

Geoffrey Chaucer was born in around 1343 in London, to a prosperous family of wine merchants. England had just been in the grip of the Black Death, a terrible plague that had killed huge numbers of people. Around a third of the country's entire population had died from the disease. Some of these had been noble courtiers in the service of King Edward III. Their sudden deaths gave ordinary people the chance to enter the king's employment.

A YOUTH AT COURT

Chaucer was one of those who took this opportunity. By the age of 17, he was a courtier, serving as a page to Prince Lionel, the king's second son. Shortly after this, Chaucer joined the king's army to fight France. England had been at war with its neighbors since 1337, when King Edward claimed the French throne. The conflict, now known as the 100 Years' War, continued right into the next century. In 1359, Chaucer took part in a mission to France. He was captured by the French and held in prison until his king paid a ransom to his captors.

During the early 1360s, Chaucer was probably a student. Soon, however, he was back in the service of the king and becoming more important. He made the first of many trips abroad as the king's diplomat. His ability to speak different languages was essential for his duties. He was fluent in French, Italian, and Latin.

In the 14th century, French was the language of the English court, as it had been since the Normans of northern France had conquered England in 1066. The language of scholars was Latin, while English was the language of the common people.

In the late 1360s, Chaucer first began to write poems. Although French poetry, with its romantic tales of love between brave knights and beautiful

Geoffrey Chaucer, by William Bell Scott
This portrait of the writer dates from the mid-19th century, when medieval art and poetry were extremely popular.

84

Master Chaucer 1400

maidens, was the favorite of the court, Chaucer preferred to write in his own language. He had no significant tradition to follow, however, since few writers considered English suitable for serious literature. Instead, he often had to work from scratch, virtually creating new forms and words.

Chaucer's early works, such as *The Romance of the Rose*, were English translations or imitations of French poetry. But later, he experimented, and his writing became more individual and original. In *Troilus and Criseyde*, for example, he mocked the French romances that he had earlier copied.

Chaucer's poetry proved very popular at court. It made English as respectable as French was for serious literature. It also helped the kind of language in which Chaucer wrote become the standard language used throughout the whole of England. Although this language—now known as Middle English—can be difficult to understand today, it is the direct ancestor of modern English.

MARRIAGE AND TRAVEL

In 1365, Chaucer made a marriage that brought him even closer to the royal family. His wife, Philippa Roet, was lady-in-waiting to the second wife of John of Gaunt. John was the third son of King Edward and, after his father, the most powerful man in England.

Chaucer continued his diplomatic trips around Europe. In 1372, he visited Italy. The country's writing must have been especially appealing to him. Two of Italy's greatest works, Boccaccio's

CANTERBURY TALES

The pinnacle of early English literature, Chaucer's famous work still delights readers 600 years after it appeared.

In Chaucer's poem, a group of religious pilgrims meet at a London tavern before setting off on a pilgrimage to Canterbury, in southeast England. The landlord of the tavern suggests that they pass the journey by telling stories as they travel: He will award a free meal to whoever provides the best tale.

In the prologue, Chaucer vividly describes each pilgrim. Many traditional characters of the period feature, from the chivalrous knight to the lusty miller and the bossy, much-married Wife of Bath (*above right*). The stories are as lively and varied as the tellers. Many

The Decameron and Dante's *Divine Comedy* (*see page 80*), were written in everyday Italian, rather than in Latin.

Meanwhile, there were problems back in England. The war with France was at a disastrous and expensive stage. French raids on English ports were disrupting trade. To pay for the war, the government increased taxes, which was unpopular with the popu-

of them have one main theme, however—the nature of relationships between the sexes.

One of the most surprising aspects of the poem is its modernity. It shows us that people 600 years ago sounded very much like people today, gossiping, worrying, and arguing about many of the same things that we do.

lation. And King Edward himself was now old and was growing senile.

This was a prosperous time for Chaucer, however. When he returned from Europe, the king put him in charge of collecting taxes on wool, England's biggest source of revenue. He spent the rest of his time writing poetry and studying everything from Greek and Roman literature to astronomy.

In 1377, King Edward III died. His ten-year-old grandson became King Richard II. A lengthy struggle developed between different factions at court to dominate the boy. In 1386, Chaucer left royal service. He may have chosen to leave to be free of the political intrigue, or he may have been forced out by opponents. Whatever the reasons, he took the break from royal duties as a chance to begin writing his masterpiece, *The Canterbury Tales*.

RETURN TO COURT

In 1389, Richard II came of age and began to assert his power. Chaucer returned to court. The king put him in charge of looking after important royal buildings, and then made him forester of one of the royal parks in Somerset, southwest England.

In 1399, Richard's cousin, Henry Bolingbroke, seized the throne, and became Henry IV. Henry was the son of John of Gaunt, to whom Chaucer had been well connected. With the new king in place, Chaucer returned to London. On October 25, 1400, he died.

MAJOR WORKS

c.1367	THE ROMANCE OF THE ROSE
c.1368	THE BOOK OF THE DUCHESS
c.1380-82	THE PARLIAMENT OF FOWLS
c.1382-85	TROILUS AND CRISEYDE
c.1386-99	THE CANTERBURY TALES

MIGUEL DE CERVANTES

Cervantes is credited as having written the first modern novel, a work translated more often than any other but the Bible. But the story of his real-life adventures might have been just as popular, had he written it.

Miguel de Cervantes Saavedra was born in 1547, in Alcalá de Henares, a city near Madrid, Spain. He was probably born on the feast day of Saint Michael—September 29—since his parents gave him the Spanish form of the saint's name.

Miguel's family had been wealthy and well connected in the past, but their prosperous days were long gone by the time he was born. His father, Rodrigo earned just enough as a barber and surgeon to support his wife, Leonor, and the couple's seven children.

The family was always on the move, chasing better fortune. They eventually settled in Madrid, in 1566. The upheaval meant that Cervantes did not get a good education. He probably had less than six years of formal schooling. He later said that he spent hours roaming the streets, educating himself by reading whatever scraps of paper he found.

The late 1560s marked Cervantes' debut as a writer. In 1567, he wrote a poem in honor of the Spanish queen,

Elizabeth de Valois. Two years later, four more of his poems appeared in a book published on Elizabeth's death. There was nothing special about the works, and, perhaps aware of his need to improve, Cervantes waited over 15 years before publishing anything again.

THE ADVENTURES BEGIN

Late in 1569, a royal order was issued for Cervantes' arrest. The decree stated that his right hand be cut off in public, and that he be exiled from Spain. It seems that the cause of all this was an illegal duel that Cervantes had fought the previous year. He did leave Spain—but managed to keep his hand.

He then went to Rome, in Italy, where he worked as a servant in the pope's court. He did not stay long in that position. In the summer of 1570, he traveled to Naples, in the south. Shortly

Portrait of Miguel de Cervantes, by Manuel Salvador Carmona
The exact date of this 18th-century engraved image of the writer is unknown.

MIGUEL DE CERVANTES
SAAVEDRA.

The Return of Don Quixote and Sancho Panza, 1909, by Sir John Gilbert
This colorful illustration shows Cervantes' idealistic hero seated on his horse, Rozinane.
His ever-loyal peasant servant, Sancho Panza, kneels beside him.

after this, a number of Italian city-states, Spain, and the pope formed an alliance of Christian forces to fight the Muslim Turks. Cervantes helped the cause by joining the Spanish navy.

The battle of Lepanto, fought in 1571 off the Greek coast, was the most famous engagement of the campaign against the Muslims. The Christians destroyed the Turkish navy, killing thousands. Despite being sick with a fever, Cervantes was a hero of the battle. He was wounded several times, and his left hand was permanently damaged. Following his recovery, he continued to fight the Turks for four more years. When he was not in battle, he was stationed in Naples, where he enjoyed the city's bustling, colorful life.

In 1575, Cervantes decided to return to Spain. But Muslim pirates attacked his ship and captured all on board.

For the next five years, Cervantes languished in a Turkish jail in Algiers, north Africa. On four occasions he tried to escape, but failed each time. In 1580, the Muslims decided to move the troublesome prisoner to the capital of Turkey, Constantinople—now Istanbul —to work as a slave. Just as Cervantes was about to leave, money arrived from his parents. It was common in those days to pay for the release of prisoners of war. The Turks eventually let him go.

Back home in Madrid, Cervantes began writing plays at a great rate—he later claimed to have written around 30 in five years, most of which were historical dramas, full of adventure and passion. Several reached the stage.

Cervantes' first novel, and his favorite work, also appeared around this time. A tale of rural life, *La Galatea*, was published in 1585. The previous year, the writer had married a woman almost 20 years younger than he—19-year-old Catalina de Salazar y Palacios. They settled in a town near Madrid.

CHANGE OF CAREER

By the late 1580s, Cervantes took a job purchasing provisions for the Spanish navy. This gave him the steady income that he now needed desperately—his father had died in 1585, leaving him the head of the family.

His time in the job was not a happy one. It often involved forcing farmers to give up provisions against their will; he was once arrested and jailed briefly for his efforts. He also tried to get supplies from the Catholic Church—as a result, he was excommunicated, which means that he was cast out of the Church.

Another change of career saw him become a tax collector—but this brought even worse luck. In 1597, he was jailed on charges of stealing other people's money. Tradition has it that he started his great novel, *Don Quixote of La Mancha*, as he lay in jail.

In 1605, the first part of this story appeared, and was an instant success. It tells of a gentleman landowner, Don Quixote, with such a passion for romance stories that he imagines himself as a medieval knight. All kinds of comic adventures befall Don Quixote and his trusted servant, Sancho Panza,

as they try to fight injustices they meet on their travels. Along the way, they discuss topics of every sort. Because of his wild and fanciful imagination, Don Quixote often loses sight of reality, but Sancho is always on hand to bring his master back to earth.

Cervantes probably wrote the book to make fun of the romances that were so popular in Spain. Instead, he created two characters that millions of people all over the world now love. Today, we use the word "quixotic," from Don Quixote's name, to describe someone who is foolishly idealistic or romantic.

FINAL YEARS

By the time the second part of Don Quixote came out in 1615, Cervantes was a famous man. He produced various other books at the end of his life. One work was a collection entitled *Exemplary Stories*—the first short stories to be written in Spanish. His last years saw another turnaround. He became increasingly pious, and decided to join a religious order. After his death at home in Madrid, in 1616, he was buried in an unmarked grave.

MAJOR WORKS

1585	LA GALATEA
1605	DON QUIXOTE (PART 1)
1613	EXEMPLARY STORIES
1614	JOURNEY OF THE PARNASSUS
1615	DON QUIXOTE (PART 2)

GLOSSARY

academy A society formed to advance the practice of art or literature.

altarpiece A religious work of art that is placed above and behind the altar in a church.

apprentice A person who learns a trade or craft by working and studying with an experienced master.

canvas A firm, closely woven cloth on which an artist paints a picture.

cartoon A detailed, full-size drawing or sketch used by an artist to prepare a painting on a wall, canvas, or panel.

classical art The painting and sculpture of ancient Greece and Rome. Also called antique, or ancient, art.

commission An order received by an artist, writer, or composer from a patron to produce a work of art, literature, or music.

composition The arrangement or organization of the various elements of a work of art, literature, or music.

courtier A person who attends or serves at a royal court.

engraving A method of making prints by cutting lines or dots into a hard surface, usually a metal plate.

fresco A wall-painting technique in which colors, or pigments, mixed with water, is applied to a layer of wet plaster. When dry, the wall and the colors are inseparable.

guilds Trade associations of artists, merchants, or craftspeople, similar to labor unions, that flourished in the Middle Ages and the Renaissance. The guilds controlled the quality of work and the training of apprentices.

landscape A kind of painting showing a view of natural scenery, such as mountains or forests.

Madonna In art, a painting or statue that represents the Virgin Mary, often with the baby Jesus and various saints.

mosaic An early form of wall or floor decoration in which tiny colored pieces of stone, marble, or glass were combined.

mythology A collection of stories about the gods or legendary heroes of a particular people.

narrative The representation in art or literature of a story or event.

naturalism A method in art or literature in which objects, places, or people are shown as they appear in nature or life, without idealization.

novel An invented story that is usually long and complex, and deals especially with human experience.

oil paint A technique developed in the 15th century in which pigments are mixed with the slow-drying and flexible medium of oil.

panel A painting on a thin, flat piece of wood.

patron A person or organization that asks an artist, writer, or composer to create a work of art, literature, or music. Usually the patron pays for the work.

perspective In art, a method used to create an illusion of depth, distance, and three-dimensional forms on a flat surface. In linear perspective, objects are shown to get smaller with distance, and parallel lines meet at a single spot on the horizon known as the "vanishing point."

Pietà A picture or statue of the Virgin Mary mourning over the body of the dead Christ.

portrait A drawing, painting, or sculpture that gives a likeness of a person and often provides an insight into his or her personality.

print A picture produced by pressing a piece of paper against a variety of inked surfaces, including engraved metal plates and wooden blocks. There are several different methods of making prints, including engraving.

prologue The preface, or introduction, to a work of literature.

Renaissance The rebirth of classical ideas that began in 14th-century Italy, lasted into the early 17th century, and led to a flowering of art and literature.

romance An invented tale, usually about love, that is based on legend and heroic adventure.

sfumato A soft, smoky effect, created by colors and tones overlapping and blending, changing very subtly from light to dark.

sitter A person who has his or her portrait produced by an artist.

sketch A rough or quick version of a picture, often produced as a trial-run for a more finished work.

style The distinctive appearance of a particular artist or writer's work of art.

symbol An object that represents something else; for example, a dove commonly symbolizes peace.

technique The way an artist uses his or her materials.

tempera A kind of paint in which pigment is dissolved in water and mixed with gum or egg white.

triptych A picture made up of three panels, usually hinged.

FURTHER READING

Arenas, Jose F. *The Key to Renaissance Art*, "Key to Art" series. Lerner Group, 1990

Chamberlain, E.R. *Florence in the Time of the Medici*. Longman Pub. Group, 1982

Chapman, Laura. *Art: Images and Ideas*, "Discover Art" series. Davis Pubns., Inc., 1992

Di Cagno. *Michelangelo*, "Masters of Art" series. Bedrick Books, 1996

Don Quixote and Sancho Panza. Adapted by Margaret Hodges. Simon & Schuster Children's, 1992

Galli, Letizia. *Mona Lisa: The Secret of the Secret Smile*. Doubleday, 1996

Harris, Nathaniel. *Renaissance Art*, "Art & Artists" series. Thomson Learning, 1994

Janson, H.W. *The History of Art*. Abrams, 1995 (standard reference)

McLanathan, Richard B. *Leonardo Da Vinci*, "First Impressions" series. Abrams, 1990

Muhlberger, Richard. *What Makes a Bruegel a Bruegel?* Viking Children's, 1993

Walker, Paul R. *The Italian Renaissance*, "World History Library." Facts on File, 1995

Wickam, Geoffrey. *Rapid Perspective*. Transatlantic Arts

INDEX

Picture Credits